MODERN CLASSICS.

1. Evangeline. / The Courtship of Miles Standish. / Favorite Poems. — LONGFELLOW.
2. Culture, Behavior, Beauty. / Books, Art, Eloquence. / Power, Wealth, Illusions. — EMERSON.
3. Nature. / Love, Friendship, Domestic Life. / Success, Greatness, Immortality. — EMERSON.
4. Snow-Bound / The Tent on the Beach. / Favorite Poems. — WHITTIER.
5. The Vision of Sir Launfal. / The Cathedral. / Favorite Poems. — LOWELL.
6. In and Out of Doors with Charles Dickens. FIELDS. / A Christmas Carol. DICKENS. / Barry Cornwall and some of his Friends. FIELDS.
7. The Ancient Mariner. / Favorite Poems. — COLERIDGE. / Favorite Poems. WORDSWORTH.
8. Undine. / Sintram. — FOUQUÉ. / Paul and Virginia. ST. PIERRE.
9. Rab and his Friends; Marjorie Fleming. / Thackeray. / John Leech. — DR. JOHN BROWN.
10. Enoch Arden. / In Memoriam. / Favorite Poems. — TENNYSON.

See page opposite inside of last cover.

Modern Classics.

THE VISION OF SIR LAUNFAL.
THE CATHEDRAL.
FAVORITE POEMS.

BY

JAMES RUSSELL LOWELL.

ILLUSTRATED.

BOSTON:
HOUGHTON, MIFFLIN AND COMPANY.
The Riverside Press, Cambridge.

The Riverside Press, Cambridge, Mass., U. S. A.
Printed by H. O. Houghton & Company.

THE VISION OF SIR LAUNFAL.

ILLUSTRATIONS.

PRELUDE TO PART FIRST.

PRELUDE.

OVER his keys the musing organist,
Beginning doubtfully and far away,
First lets his fingers wander as they list,
And builds a bridge from Dreamland for his lay:
Then, as the touch of his loved instrument
Gives hope and fervor, nearer draws his theme,

First guessed by faint auroral flushes sent
Along the wavering vista of his dream.

Not only around our infancy
Doth heaven with all its splendors lie;
Daily, with souls that cringe and plot,
We Sinais climb and know it not.
Over our manhood bend the skies;
Against our fallen and traitor lives
The great winds utter prophecies;
With our faint hearts the mountain strives;
Its arms outstretched, the druid wood

Waits with its benedicite;
And to our age's drowsy blood
Still shouts the inspiring sea.

Earth gets its price for what Earth gives us;
The beggar is taxed for a corner to die in,
The priest hath his fee who comes and shrives us,
We bargain for the graves we lie in;
At the Devil's booth are all things sold,
Each ounce of dross costs its ounce of gold;

For a cap and bells our lives we pay,
Bubbles we earn with a whole soul's tasking:
'T is heaven alone that is given away,
'T is only God may be had for the asking;
No price is set on the lavish summer,
June may be had by the poorest comer.

And what is so rare as a day in June?
Then, if ever, come perfect days;
Then Heaven tries the earth if it be in tune,

And over it softly her warm ear lays:
Whether we look, or whether we listen,
We hear life murmur, or see it glisten;
Every clod feels a stir of might,
An instinct within it that reaches and towers,
And, groping blindly above it for light,
Climbs to a soul in grass and flowers;
The flush of life may well be seen
Thrilling back over hills and valleys;
The cowslip startles in meadows green,
The buttercup catches the sun in its chalice,

And there's never a leaf nor a blade too mean
  To be some happy creature's palace;
The little bird sits at his door in the sun,
  Atilt like a blossom among the leaves,
And lets his illumined being o'errun
  With the deluge of summer it receives;
His mate feels the eggs beneath her wings,
And the heart in her dumb breast flutters and sings;
He sings to the wide world, and she to her nest, —
In the nice ear of Nature which song is the best?

Now is the high-tide of the year,
And whatever of life hath ebbed away
Comes flooding back with a ripply cheer,
Into every bare inlet and creek and bay;
Now the heart is so full that a drop overfills it,
We are happy now because God wills it;
No matter how barren the past may have been,
'T is enough for us now that the leaves are green;
We sit in the warm shade and feel right well

How the sap creeps up and the blossoms
swell;
We may shut our eyes, but we cannot
help knowing
That skies are clear and grass is growing;
The breeze comes whispering in our ear,
That dandelions are blossoming near,
That maize has sprouted, that streams
are flowing,
That the river is bluer than the sky,
That the robin is plastering his house
hard by;
And if the breeze kept the good news back,

For other couriers we should not lack;
We could guess it all by yon heifer's lowing, —
And hark! how clear bold chanticleer,
Warmed with the new wine of the year,
Tells all in his lusty crowing!

Joy comes, grief goes, we know not how;
Everything is happy now,
Everything is upward striving;
'T is as easy now for the heart to be true
As for grass to be green or skies to be blue, —

'T is the natural way of living:
Who knows whither the clouds have fled?
In the unscarred heaven they leave no wake;
And the eyes forget the tears they have shed.
The heart forgets its sorrow and ache;
The soul partakes the season's youth,
And the sulphurous rifts of passion and woe
Lie deep 'neath a silence pure and smooth,
Like burnt-out craters healed with snow.
What wonder if Sir Launfal now
Remembered the keeping of his vow?

THE VISION
OF
Sir Launfal.

PART FIRST.

PART FIRST.

I.

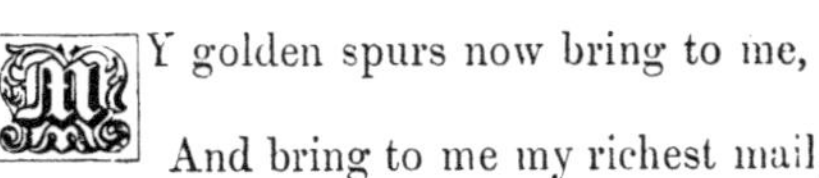

MY golden spurs now bring to me,
  And bring to me my richest mail,
For to-morrow I go over land and sea
  In search of the Holy Grail;
Shall never a bed for me be spread,
Nor shall a pillow be under my head,
Till I begin my vow to keep;

Here on the rushes will I sleep,
And perchance there may come a vision
true
Ere day create the world anew."
Slowly Sir Launfal's eyes grew dim,
Slumber fell like a cloud on him,
And into his soul the vision flew.

II.

The crows flapped over by twos and threes,
In the pool drowsed the cattle up to their
knees,
The little birds sang as if it were

The one day of summer in all the
year,
And the very leaves seemed to sing on the
trees:
The castle alone in the landscape lay
Like an outpost of winter, dull and gray:
'T was the proudest hall in the North
Countree,
And never its gates might opened be,
Save to lord or lady of high degree;
Summer besieged it on every side,
But the churlish stone her assaults defied;
She could not scale the chilly wall,

Though round it for leagues her pavilions
tall
Stretched left and right,
Over the hills and out of sight;
Green and broad was every tent,
And out of each a murmur went
Till the breeze fell off at night.

III.

The drawbridge dropped with a surly
clang,
And through the dark arch a charger sprang,
Bearing Sir Launfal, the maiden knight,

In his gilded mail, that flamed so bright
It seemed the dark castle had gathered all
Those shafts the fierce sun had shot over its wall
In his siege of three hundred summers long,
And, binding them all in one blazing sheaf,
Had cast them forth: so, young and strong,
And lightsome as a locust-leaf,
Sir Launfal flashed forth in his unscarred mail,
To seek in all climes for the Holy Grail.

IV.

It was morning on hill and stream and tree,
And morning in the young knight's heart;
Only the castle moodily
Rebuffed the gifts of the sunshine free,
And gloomed by itself apart;
The season brimmed all other things up
Full as the rain fills the pitcher-plant's cup.

V.

As Sir Launfal made morn through the darksome gate,

He was 'ware of a leper, crouched by the
same,
Who begged with his hand and moaned as
he sate;
And a loathing over Sir Launfal came;
The sunshine went out of his soul with a
thrill,
The flesh 'neath his armor 'gan shrink
and crawl,
And midway its leap his heart stood still
Like a frozen waterfall;
For this man, so foul and bent of stature,
Rasped harshly against his dainty nature,

And seemed the one blot on the summer
morn, —
So he tossed him a piece of gold in scorn.

VI.

The leper raised not the gold from the dust:
"Better to me the poor man's crust,
Better the blessing of the poor,
Though I turn me empty from his door;
That is no true alms which the hand can
hold;
He gives nothing but worthless gold
Who gives from a sense of duty;

But he who gives a slender mite,
And gives to that which is out of sight,
  That thread of the all-sustaining Beauty
Which runs through all and doth all
    unite, —
The hand cannot clasp the whole of his
    alms,
The heart outstretches its eager palms,
For a god goes with it and makes it store
To the soul that was starving in darkness
    before."

PRELUDE TO PART SECOND.

PRELUDE.

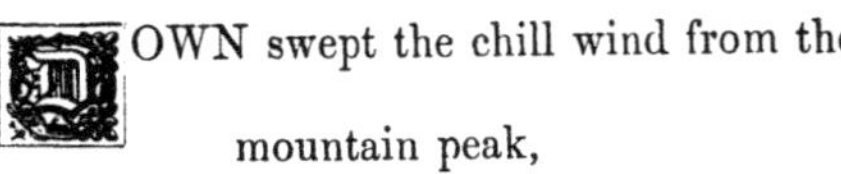

OWN swept the chill wind from the
mountain peak,
From the snow five thousand summers
old;
On open wold and hill-top bleak
It had gathered all the cold,
And whirled it like sleet on the wanderer's
cheek;

It carried a shiver everywhere
From the unleafed boughs and pastures
bare;
The little brook heard it and built a roof
'Neath which he could house him, winter-
proof;
All night by the white stars' frosty gleams
He groined his arches and matched his
beams;
Slender and clear were his crystal spars
As the lashes of light that trim the stars:
He sculptured every summer delight
In his halls and chambers out of sight;

Sometimes his tinkling waters slipt
Down through a frost-leaved forest-crypt,
Long, sparkling aisles of steel-stemmed
trees
Bending to counterfeit a breeze;
Sometimes the roof no fretwork knew
But silvery mosses that downward grew;
Sometimes it was carved in sharp relief
With quaint arabesques of ice-fern leaf;
Sometimes it was simply smooth and clear
For the gladness of heaven to shine through,
and here
He had caught the nodding bulrush-tops

And hung them thickly with diamond drops,
Which crystalled the beams of moon and
sun,
And made a star of every one:
No mortal builder's most rare device
Could match this winter-palace of ice;
'T was as if every image that mirrored lay
In his depths serene through the summer
day,
Each fleeting shadow of earth and sky,
Lest the happy model should be lost,
Had been mimicked in fairy masonry
By the elfin builders of the frost.

Within the hall are song and laughter,
The cheeks of Christmas glow red and jolly,
And sprouting is every corbel and rafter
With lightsome green of ivy and holly;
Through the deep gulf of the chimney wide
Wallows the Yule-log's roaring tide;
The broad flame-pennons droop and flap
And belly and tug as a flag in the wind;
Like a locust shrills the imprisoned sap,
Hunted to death in its galleries blind;
And swift little troops of silent sparks,

Now pausing, now scattering away as in
fear,
Go threading the soot-forest's tangled darks
Like herds of startled deer.

But the wind without was eager and sharp,
Of Sir Launfal's gray hair it makes a harp
And rattles and wrings
The icy strings,
Singing, in dreary monotone,
A Christmas carol of its own,
Whose burden still, as he might guess,
Was "Shelterless, shelterless, shelterless!"

The voice of the seneschal flared like a
torch
As he shouted the wanderer away from the
porch,
And he sat in the gateway and saw all night
The great hall-fire, so cheery and bold,
Through the window-slits of the castle
old,
Build out its piers of ruddy light
Against the drift of the cold.

THE VISION

OF

Sir Launfal.

PART SECOND.

PART SECOND.

I.

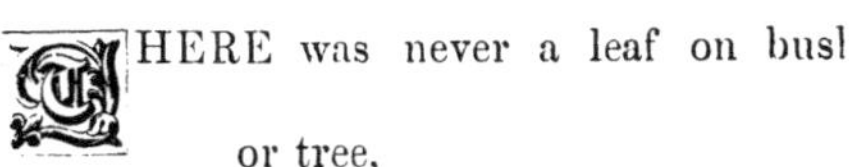

THERE was never a leaf on bush or tree,
The bare boughs rattled shudderingly;
The river was dumb and could not speak,
For the weaver Winter its shroud had spun;
A single crow on the tree-top bleak

From his shining feathers shed off the
cold sun;
Again it was morning, but shrunk and cold,
As if her veins were sapless and old,
And she rose up decrepitly
For a last dim look at earth and sea.

II.

Sir Launfal turned from his own hard gate,
For another heir in his earldom sate;
An old, bent man, worn out and frail,
He came back from seeking the Holy Grail;
Little he recked of his earldom's loss,

No more on his surcoat was blazoned the
cross,
But deep in his soul the sign he wore,
The badge of the suffering and the poor.

III.

Sir Launfal's raiment thin and spare
Was idle mail 'gainst the barbéd air,
For it was just at the Christmas time;
So he mused, as he sat, of a sunnier clime,
And sought for shelter from cold and snow
In the light and warmth of long-ago;
He sees the snake-like caravan crawl

O'er the edge of the desert, black and small,
Then nearer and nearer, till, one by one,
He can count the camels in the sun,
As over the red-hot sands they pass
To where, in its slender necklace of grass,
The little spring laughed and leapt in the
shade,
And with its own self like an infant played,
And waved its signal of palms.

IV.

"For Christ's sweet sake, I beg an alms"; —
The happy camels may reach the spring,

But Sir Launfal sees naught save the grew-
some thing,
The leper, lank as the rain-blanched bone,
That cowers beside him, a thing as lone
And white as the ice-isles of Northern seas
In the desolate horror of his disease.

V.

And Sir Launfal said, "I behold in thee
An image of Him who died on the tree;
Thou also hast had thy crown of thorns, —
Thou also hast had the world's buffets and
and scorns, —

And to thy life were not denied
The wounds in the hands and feet and side:
Mild Mary's Son, acknowledge me;
Behold, through him, I give to thee!"

VI.

Then the soul of the leper stood up in his eyes
And looked at Sir Launfal, and straightway he
Remembered in what a haughtier guise
He had flung an alms to leprosie,

When he girt his young life up in gilded
mail
And set forth in search of the Holy Grail.
The heart within him was ashes and
dust;
He parted in twain his single crust,
He broke the ice on the streamlet's brink,
And gave the leper to eat and drink,
'T was a mouldy crust of coarse brown
bread,
'T was water out of a wooden bowl,—
Yet with fine wheaten bread was the leper
fed,

And 't was red wine he drank with his
thirsty soul.

VII.

As Sir Launfal mused with a downcast face,
A light shone round about the place;
The leper no longer crouched at his side,
But stood before him glorified,
Shining and tall and fair and straight
As the pillar that stood by the Beautiful
Gate, —
Himself the Gate whereby men can
Enter the temple of God in Man.

VIII.

His words were shed softer than leaves from
the pine,
And they fell on Sir Launfal as snows on
the brine,
That mingle their softness and quiet in
one
With the shaggy unrest they float down
upon;
And the voice that was calmer than silence
said,
"Lo, it is I, be not afraid!

In many climes, without avail,
Thou hast spent thy life for the Holy Grail;
Behold, it is here, — this cup which thou
Didst fill at the streamlet for me but now;
This crust is my body broken for thee,
This water His blood that died on the tree;
The Holy Supper is kept, indeed,
In whatso we share with another's need;
Not what we give, but what we share,
For the gift without the giver is bare;
Who gives himself with his alms feeds three, —
Himself, his hungering neighbor, and me."

IX.

Sir Launfal awoke as from a swound:
"The Grail in my castle here is found!
Hang my idle armor up on the wall,
Let it be the spider's banquet-hall;
He must be fenced with stronger mail
Who would seek and find the Holy Grail."

X.

The castle-gate stands open now,
And the wanderer is welcome to the hall!

As the hangbird is to the elm-tree bough;
No longer scowl the turrets tall,
The Summer's long siege at last is o'er;
When the first poor outcast went in at the
door,
She entered with him in disguise,
And mastered the fortress by surprise;
There is no spot she loves so well on
ground,
She lingers and smiles there the whole year
round;
The meanest serf on Sir Launfal's land
Has hall and bower at his command;

And there 's no poor man in the North
Countree
But is lord of the earldom as much as he.

NOTE.

NOTE.

ACCORDING to the mythology of the Romancers, the San Greal, or Holy Grail, was the cup out of which Jesus partook of the last supper with his disciples. It was brought into England by Joseph of Arimathea, and remained there, an object of pilgrimage and adoration, for many years in the keeping of his lineal descendants. It was incumbent upon those who had charge of it to be chaste in thought, word, and deed; but one of the keepers having broken this condition, the Holy Grail disappeared. From that time it was a favorite enterprise of the knights of Arthur's court to go in search of it. Sir Galahad was at last successful in finding it, as may be read in the seventeenth book of the Romance of King Arthur. Tennyson has made Sir Galahad the subject of one of the most exquisite of his poems.

The plot (if I may give that name to anything so slight) of the foregoing poem is my own, and, to serve its purposes, I have enlarged the circle of competition in search of the miraculous cup in such a manner as to include, not only other persons than the heroes of the Round Table, but also a period of time subsequent to the date of King Arthur's reign.

THE CATHEDRAL.

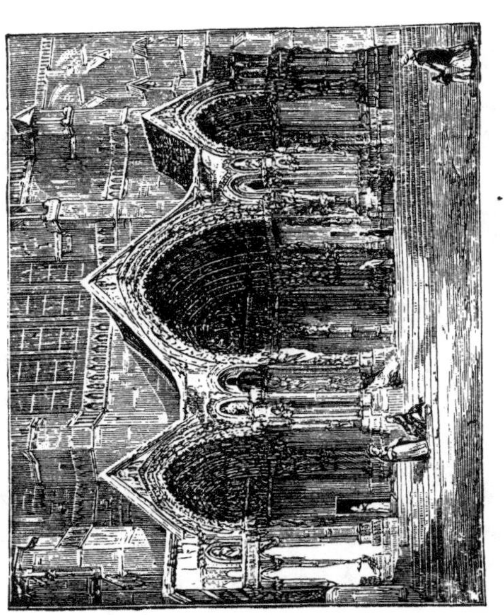

CONTENTS.

Οὐδὲν σοφιζώμεσθα τοῖσι δαίμοισιν.
Πατρίους παραδοχὰς, ἅς θ' ὁμήλικας χρόνῳ
Κεκτήμεθ', οὐδεὶς αὐτὰ καταβαλεῖ λόγος,
Οὐδ' ἢν δι' ἄκρων τὸ σορὸν εὕρηται φρενῶν

THE CATHEDRAL.

AR through the memory shines a happy
day,
Cloudless of care, down-shod to every sense,
And simply perfect from its own resource,
As to a bee the new campanula's
Illuminate seclusion swung in air.
Such days are not the prey of setting suns,
Nor ever blurred with mist of after-thought;
Like words made magical by poets dead,
Wherein the music of all meaning is
The sense hath garnered or the soul divined,

They mingle with our life's ethereal part,
Sweetening and gathering sweetness evermore,

By Beauty's franchise disenthralled of time.
I can recall, nay, they are present still,
Parts of myself, the perfume of my mind,
Days that seem farther off than Homer's now
Ere yet the child had loudened to the boy,
And I, recluse from playmates, found perforce
Companionship in things that not denied
Nor granted wholly; as is Nature's wont,
Who, safe in uncontaminate reserve,
Lets us mistake our longing for her love,
And mocks with various echo of ourselves.

These first sweet frauds upon our consciousness,
That blend the sensual with its imaged world,

These virginal cognitions, gifts of morn,
Ere life grow noisy, and slower-footed thought
Can overtake the rapture of the sense,
To thrust between ourselves and what we feel,
Have something in them secretly divine.
Vainly the eye, once schooled to serve the brain,
With pains deliberate studies to renew
The ideal vision: second-thoughts are prose;
For Beauty's acme hath a term as brief
As the wave's poise before it break in pearl.
Our own breath dims the mirror of the sense,
Looking too long and closely: at a flash
We snatch the essential grace of meaning out.
And that first passion beggars all behind,
Heirs of a tamer transport prepossessed.
Who, seeing once, has truly seen again

The gray vague of unsympathizing sea
That dragged his Fancy from her moorings back
To shores inhospitable of eldest time,
Till blank foreboding of earth-gendered power,
Pitiless seignories in the elements,
Omnipotences blind that darkling smite,
Misgave him, and repaganized the world?
Yet, by some subtler touch of sympathy,
These primal apprehensions, dimly stirred,
Perplex the eye with pictures from within.
This hath made poets dream of lives foregone
In worlds fantastical, more fair than ours;
So Memory cheats us, glimpsing half-revealed.
Even as I write she tries her wonted spell
In that continuous redbreast boding rain:
The bird I hear sings not from yonder elm;
But the flown ecstasy my childhood heard

Is vocal in my mind, renewed by him,
Haply made sweeter by the accumulate thrill
That threads my undivided life and steals
A pathos from the years and graves between.

I know not how it is with other men,
Whom I but guess, deciphering myself;
For me, once felt is so felt nevermore.
The fleeting relish at sensation's brim
Had in it the best ferment of the wine.
One spring I knew as never any since:
All night the surges of the warm southwest
Boomed intermittent through the shuddering
elms,
And brought a morning from the Gulf adrift,
Omnipotent with sunshine, whose quick charm
Startled with crocuses the sullen turf
And wiled the bluebird to his whiff of song:

One summer hour abides, what time I perched,
Dappled with noonday, under simmering leaves,
And pulled the pulpy oxhearts, while aloof
An oriole clattered and the robins shrilled,
Denouncing me an alien and a thief:
One morn of autumn lords it o'er the rest,
When in the lane I watched the ash-leaves fall,
Balancing softly earthward without wind,
Or twirling with directer impulse down
On those fallen yesterday, now barbed with frost,
While I grew pensive with the pensive year:
And once I learned how marvellous winter was,
When past the fence-rails, downy-gray with rime,
I creaked adventurous o'er the spangled crust
That made familiar fields seem far and strange

As those stark wastes that whiten endlessly
In ghastly solitude about the pole,
And gleam relentless to the unsetting sun:
Instant the candid chambers of my brain
Were painted with these sovran images;
And later visions seem but copies pale
From those unfading frescos of the past,
Which I, young savage, in my age of flint,
Gazed at, and dimly felt a power in me
Parted from Nature by the joy in her
That doubtfully revealed me to myself.
Thenceforward I must stand outside the gate;
And paradise was paradise the more,
Known once and barred against satiety.

What we call Nature, all outside ourselves,
Is but our own conceit of what we see,
Our own reaction upon what we feel;

The world 's a woman to our shifting mood,
Feeling with us, or making due pretence;
And therefore we the more persuade ourselves
To make all things our thought's confederates,
Conniving with us in whate'er we dream.
So when our Fancy seeks analogies,
Though she have hidden what she after finds,
She loves to cheat herself with feigned surprise.
I find my own complexion everywhere:
No rose, I doubt, was ever, like the first,
A marvel to the bush it dawned upon,
The rapture of its life made visible,
The mystery of its yearning realized,
As the first babe to the first woman born;
No falcon ever felt delight of wings
As when, an eyas, from the stolid cliff
Loosing himself, he followed his high heart
To swim on sunshine, masterless as wind;

And I believe the brown Earth takes delight
In the new snowdrop looking back at her,
To think that by some vernal alchemy
It could transmute her darkness into pearl;
What is the buxom peony after that,
With its coarse constancy of hoyden blush?
What the full summer to that wonder new?

But, if in nothing else, in us there is
A sense fastidious hardly reconciled
To the poor makeshifts of life's scenery,
Where the same slide must double all its parts,
Shoved in for Tarsus and hitched back for Tyre.
I blame not in the soul this daintiness,
Rasher of surfeit than a humming-bird,
In things indifferent by sense purveyed;
It argues her an immortality
And dateless incomes of experience,

This unthrift housekeeping that will not brook
A dish warmed-over at the feast of life,
And finds Twice stale, served with whatever sauce.
Nor matters much how it may go with me
Who dwell in Grub Street and am proud to drudge
Where men, my betters, wet their crust with tears:
Use can make sweet the peach's shady side,
That only by reflection tastes of sun.

But she, my Princess, who will sometimes deign
My garret to illumine till the walls,
Narrow and dingy, scrawled with hackneyed thought
(Poor Richard slowly elbowing Plato out),
Dilate and drape themselves with tapestries

Nausikaa might have stooped o'er, while, between,
Mirrors, effaced in their own clearness, send
Her only image on through deepening deeps
With endless repercussion of delight, —
Bringer of life, witching each sense to soul,
That sometimes almost gives me to believe
I might have been a poet, gives at least
A brain desaxonized, an ear that makes
Music where none is, and a keener pang
Of exquisite surmise outleaping thought, —
Her will I pamper in her luxury:
No crumpled rose-leaf of too careless choice
Shall bring a northern nightmare to her dreams,
Vexing with sense of exile; hers shall be
The invitiate firstlings of experience,
Vibrations felt but once and felt lifelong:
O, more than half-way turn that Grecian front

Upon me, while with self-rebuke I spell,
On the plain fillet that confines thy hair
In conscious bounds of seeming unconstraint,
The *Naught in overplus*, thy race's badge!

One feast for her I secretly designed
In that Old World so strangely beautiful
To us the disinherited of eld, —
A day at Chartres, with no soul beside
To roil with pedant prate my joy serene
And make the minster shy of confidence.
I went, and, with the Saxon's pious care,
First ordered dinner at the pea-green inn,
The flies and I its only customers,
Till by and by there came two Englishmen,
Who made me feel, in their engaging way,
I was a poacher on their self-preserve,
Intent constructively on lese-anglicism,

To them (in those old razor-ridden days)
My beard translated me to hostile French;
So they, desiring guidance in the town,
Half condescended to my baser sphere,
And, clubbing in one mess their lack of phrase,
Set their best man to grapple with the Gaul.
"Esker vous ate a nabitang?" he asked;
"I never ate one; are they good?" asked I;
Whereat they stared, then laughed, and we
were friends,
The seas, the wars, the centuries interposed,
Abolished in the truce of common speech
And mutual comfort of the mother-tongue.
Like escaped convicts of Propriety,
They furtively partook the joys of men,
Glancing behind when buzzed some louder fly.

Eluding these, I loitered through the town,

With hope to take my minster unawares
In its grave solitude of memory.
A pretty burgh, and such as Fancy loves
For bygone grandeurs, faintly rumorous now
Upon the mind's horizon, as of storm
Brooding its dreamy thunders far aloof,
That mingle with our mood, but not disturb.
Its once grim bulwarks, tamed to lovers' walks,
Look down unwatchful on the sliding Eure,
Whose listless leisure suits the quiet place,
Lisping among his shallows homelike sounds
At Concord and by Bankside heard before.
Chance led me to a public pleasure-ground,
Where I grew kindly with the merry groups,
And blessed the Frenchman for his simple art
Of being domestic in the light of day.
His language has no word, we growl, for Home;
But he can find a fireside in the sun,

Play with his child, make love, and shriek his
mind,
By throngs of strangers undisprivacied.
He makes his life a public gallery,
Nor feels himself till what he feels comes back
In manifold reflection from without;
While we, each pore alert with consciousness,
Hide our best selves as we had stolen them,
And each bystander a detective were,
Keen-eyed for every chink of undisguise.

So, musing o'er the problem which was best, —
A life wide-windowed, shining all abroad,
Or curtains drawn to shield from sight pro
fane
The rites we pay to the mysterious I, —
With outward senses furloughed and head
bowed

I followed some fine instinct in my feet,
Till, to unbend me from the loom of thought,
Looking up suddenly, I found mine eyes
Confronted with the minster's vast repose.
Silent and gray as forest-leaguered cliff
Left inland by the ocean's slow retreat,
That hears afar the breeze-borne rote and longs,
Remembering shocks of surf that clomb and fell,
Spume-sliding down the baffled decuman,
It rose before me, patiently remote
From the great tides of life it breasted once,
Hearing the noise of men as in a dream.
I stood before the triple northern port,
Where dedicated shapes of saints and kings,
Stern faces bleared with immemorial watch,
Looked down benignly grave and seemed to say,

Ye come and go incessant; we remain
Safe in the hallowed quiets of the past;
Be reverent, ye who flit and are forgot,
Of faith so nobly realized as this.
I seem to have heard it said by learnëd folk
Who drench you with æsthetics till you feel
As if all beauty were a ghastly bore,
The faucet to let loose a wash of words,
That Gothic is not Grecian, therefore worse;
But, being convinced by much experiment
How little inventiveness there is in man,
Grave copier of copies, I give thanks
For a new relish, careless to inquire
My pleasure's pedigree, if so it please,
Nobly, I mean, nor renegade to art.
The Grecian gluts me with its perfectness,
Unanswerable as Euclid, self-contained,
The one thing finished in this hasty world,

Forever finished, though the barbarous pit,
Fanatical on hearsay, stamp and shout
As if a miracle could be encored.
But ah! this other, this that never ends,
Still climbing, luring fancy still to climb,
As full of morals half-divined as life,
Graceful, grotesque, with ever new surprise
Of hazardous caprices sure to please,
Heavy as nightmare, airy-light as fern,
Imagination's very self in stone!
With one long sigh of infinite release
From pedantries past, present, or to come,
I looked, and owned myself a happy Goth.
Your blood is mine, ye architects of dream,
Builders of aspiration incomplete,
So more consummate, souls self-confident,
Who felt your own thought worthy of record
In monumental pomp! No Grecian drop

Rebukes these veins that leap with kindred
thrill,
After long exile, to the mother-tongue.

Ovid in Pontus, puling for his Rome
Of men invirile and disnatured dames
That poison sucked from the Attic bloom decayed,
Shrank with a shudder from the blue-eyed race
Whose force rough-handed should renew the
world,
And from the dregs of Romulus express
Such wine as Dante poured, or he who blew
Roland's vain blast, or sang the Campeador
In verse that clanks like armor in the charge, —
Homeric juice, if brimmed in Odin's horn.
And they could build, if not the columned fane
That from the height gleamed seaward many-hued,

Something more friendly with their ruder skies:
The gray spire, molten now in driving mist,
Now lulled with the incommunicable blue;
The carvings touched to meanings new with
snow,
Or commented with fleeting grace of shade;
The statues, motley as man's memory,
Partial as that, so mixed of true and false,
History and Legend meeting with a kiss
Across this bound-mark where their realms
confine;
The painted windows, freaking gloom with
glow,
Dusking the sunshine which they seem to cheer,
Meet symbol of the senses and the soul;
And the whole pile, grim with the Northman's
thought
Of life and death, and doom, life's equal fee, —

These were before me: and I gazed abashed,
Child of an age that lectures, not creates,
Plastering our swallow-nests on the awful Past,
And twittering round the work of larger men,
As we had builded what we but deface.
Far up the great bells wallowed in delight,
Tossing their clangors o'er the heedless town,
To call the worshippers who never came,
Or women mostly, in loath twos and threes.
I entered, reverent of whatever shrine
Guards piety and solace for my kind
Or gives the soul a moment's truce of God,
And shared decorous in the ancient rite
My sterner fathers held idolatrous.
The service over, I was tranced in thought:
Solemn the deepening vaults, and most to me,
Fresh from the fragile realm of deal and paint,
Or brick mock-pious with a marble front;

Solemn the lift of high-embowered roof,
The clustered stems that spread in boughs dis-leaved,
Through which the organ blew a dream of storm, —
Though not more potent to sublime with awe
And shut the heart up in tranquillity,
Than aisles to me familiar that o'erarch
The conscious silences of brooding woods,
Centurial shadows, cloisters of the elk:
Yet here was sense of undefined regret,
Irreparable loss, uncertain what:
Was all this grandeur but anachronism, —
A shell divorced of its informing life,
Where the priest housed him like a hermit-crab,
An alien to that faith of elder days
That gathered round it this fair shape of stone?
Is old Religion but a spectre now,

Haunting the solitude of darkened minds,
Mocked out of memory by the sceptic day?
Is there no corner safe from peeping Doubt,
Since Gutenberg made thought cosmopolite
And stretched electric threads from mind to
mind?
Nay, did Faith build this wonder? or did Fear,
That makes a fetish and misnames it God
(Blockish or metaphysic, matters not),
Contrive this coop to shut its tyrant in,
Appeased with playthings, that he might not
harm?

I turned and saw a beldame on her knees;
With eyes astray, she told mechanic beads
Before some shrine of saintly womanhood,
Bribed intercessor with the far-off Judge:
Such my first thought, by kindlier soon re-
buked,

Pleading for whatsoever touches life
With upward impulse: be He nowhere else,
God is in all that liberates and lifts,
In all that humbles, sweetens, and consoles:
Blessëd the natures shored on every side
With landmarks of hereditary thought!
Thrice happy they that wander not lifelong
Beyond near succor of the household faith,
The guarded fold that shelters, not confines!
Their steps find patience in familiar paths,
Printed with hope by loved feet gone before
Of parent, child, or lover, glorified
By simple magic of dividing Time.
My lids were moistened as the woman knelt,
And — was it will, or some vibration faint
Of sacred Nature, deeper than the will? —
My heart occultly felt itself in hers,
Through mutual intercession gently leagued.

Or was it not mere sympathy of brain?
A sweetness intellectually conceived
In simpler creeds to me impossible?
A juggle of that pity for ourselves
In others, which puts on such pretty masks
And snares self-love with bait of charity?
Something of all it might be, or of none:
Yet for a moment I was snatched away
And had the evidence of things not seen;
For one rapt moment; then it all came back,
This age that blots out life with question-marks,
This nineteenth century with its knife and glass
That make thought physical, and thrust far off
The Heaven, so neighborly with man of old,
To voids sparse-sown with alienated stars.

'T is irrecoverable, that ancient faith,
Homely and wholesome, suited to the time,

With rod or candy for child-minded men:
No theologic tube, with lens on lens
Of syllogism transparent, brings it near, —
At best resolving some new nebula,
Or blurring some fixed-star of hope to mist.
Science was Faith once; Faith were Science now,
Would she but lay her bow and arrows by
And arm her with the weapons of the time.
Nothing that keeps thought out is safe from thought.
For there 's no virgin-fort but self-respect,
And Truth defensive hath lost hold on God.
Shall we treat Him as if He were a child
That knew not His own purpose? nor dare trust
The Rock of Ages to their chemic tests,
Lest some day the all-sustaining base divine
Should fail from under us, dissolved in gas?

The armëd eye that with a glance discerns
In a dry blood-speck between ox and man,
Stares helpless at this miracle called life,
This shaping potency behind the egg,
This circulation swift of deity,
Where suns and systems inconspicuous float
As the poor blood-disks in our mortal veins.
Each age must worship its own thought of God,
More or less earthy, clarifying still
With subsidence continuous of the dregs;
Nor saint nor sage could fix immutably
The fluent image of the unstable Best,
Still changing in their very hands that wrought:
To-day's eternal truth To-morrow proved
Frail as frost-landscapes on a window-pane.
Meanwhile Thou smiledst, inaccessible,
At Thought's own substance made a cage for
Thought,

And Truth locked fast with her own master-key;
Nor didst Thou reck what image man might make
Of his own shadow on the flowing world;
The climbing instinct was enough for Thee.
Or wast Thou, then, an ebbing tide that left
Strewn with dead miracle those eldest shores,
For men to dry, and dryly lecture on,
Thyself thenceforth incapable of flood?
Idle who hopes with prophets to be snatched
By virtue in their mantles left below;
Shall the soul live on other men's report,
Herself a pleasing fable of herself?
Man cannot be God's outlaw if he would,
Nor so abscond him in the caves of sense
But Nature still shall search some crevice out
With messages of splendor from that Source

Which, dive he, soar he, baffles still and lures.
This life were brutish did we not sometimes
Have intimation clear of wider scope,
Hints of occasion infinite, to keep
The soul alert with noble discontent
And onward yearnings of unstilled desire;
Fruitless, except we now and then divined
A mystery of Purpose, gleaming through
The secular confusions of the world,
Whose will we darkly accomplish, doing ours.
No man can think nor in himself perceive,
Sometimes at waking, in the street sometimes,
Or on the hillside, always unforewarned,
A grace of being, finer than himself,
That beckons and is gone, — a larger life
Upon his own impinging, with swift glimpse
Of spacious circles luminous with mind,
To which the ethereal substance of his own

Seems but gross cloud to make that visible,
Touched to a sudden glory round the edge.
Who that hath known these visitations fleet
Would strive to make them trite and ritual?
I, that still pray at morning and at eve,
Loving those roots that feed us from the past,
And prizing more than Plato things I learned
At that best academe, a mother's knee,
Thrice in my life perhaps have truly prayed,
Thrice, stirred below my conscious self, have felt
That perfect disenthralment which is God;
Nor know I which to hold worst enemy, —
Him who on speculation's windy waste
Would turn me loose, stript of the raiment warm
By Faith contrived against our nakedness,
Or him who, cruel-kind, would fain obscure,

With painted saints and paraphrase of God ;
The soul's east-window of divine surprise.
Where others worship I but look and long ;
For, though not recreant to my fathers' faith,
Its forms to me are weariness, and most
That drony vacuum of compulsory prayer,
Still pumping phrases for the Ineffable,
Though all the valves of memory gasp and wheeze.
Words that have drawn transcendent meanings up
From the best passion of all bygone time,
Steeped through with tears of triumph and remorse,
Sweet with all sainthood, cleansed in martyr-fires,
Can they, so consecrate and so inspired,
By repetition wane to vexing wind ?

Alas! we cannot draw habitual breath
In the thin air of life's supremer heights,
We cannot make each meal a sacrament,
Nor with our tailors be disbodied souls, —
We men, too conscious of earth's comedy,
Who see two sides, with our posed selves debate,
And only for great stakes can be sublime!
Let us be thankful when, as I do here,
We can read Bethel on a pile of stones,
And, seeing where God *has* been, trust in Him.

Brave Peter Fischer there in Nuremberg,
Moulding Saint Sebald's miracles in bronze,
Put saint and stander-by in that quaint garb
Familiar to him in his daily walk,
Not doubting God could grant a miracle

Then and in Nuremberg, if so He would;
But never artist for three hundred years
Hath dared the contradiction ludicrous
Of supernatural in modern clothes.
Perhaps the deeper faith that is to come
Will see God rather in the strenuous doubt,
Than in the creed held as an infant's hand
Holds purposeless whatso is placed therein.

Say it is drift, not progress, none the less,
With the old sextant of the fathers' creed,
We shape our courses by new-risen stars,
And, still lip-loyal to what once was truth,
Smuggle new meanings under ancient names,
Unconscious perverts of the Jesuit, Time.
Change is the mask that all Continuance wears
To keep us youngsters harmlessly amused;
Meanwhile, some ailing or more watchful child,

Sitting apart, sees the old eyes gleam out,
Stern, and yet soft with humorous pity too.
Whilere, men burnt men for a doubtful point,
As if the mind were quenchable with fire,
And Faith danced round them with her war-
paint on,
Devoutly savage as an Iroquois;
Now Calvin and Servetus at one board
Snuff in grave sympathy a milder roast,
And o'er their claret settle Comte unread.
Fagot and stake were desperately sincere:
Our cooler martyrdoms are done in types;
And flames that shine in controversial eyes
Burn out no brains but his who kindles them.
This is no age to get cathedrals built:
Did God, then, wait for one in Bethlehem?
Worst is not yet: lo, where his coming looms,
Of Earth's anarchic children latest born,

Democracy, a Titan who hath learned
To laugh at Jove's old-fashioned thunder-
bolts, —
Could he not also forge them, if he would?
He, better skilled, with solvents merciless,
Loosened in air and borne on every wind,
Saps unperceived: the calm Olympian height
Of ancient order feels its bases yield,
And pale gods glance for help to gods as pale.
What will be left of good or worshipful,
Of spiritual secrets, mysteries,
Of fair Religion's guarded heritage,
Heirlooms of soul, passed downward unpro-
faned
From eldest Ind? This Western giant coarse
Scorning refinements which he lacks himself,
Loves not nor heeds the ancestral hierarchies,
Each rank dependent on the next above

In orderly gradation fixed as fate.
King by mere manhood, nor allowing aught
Of holier unction than the sweat of toil;
In his own strength sufficient; called to solve,
On the rough edges of society,
Problems long sacred to the choicer few,
And improvise what elsewhere men receive
As gifts of Deity; tough foundling reared
Where every man 's his own Melchisedek,
How make him reverent of a King of kings?
Or Judge self-made, executor of laws
By him not first discussed and voted on?
For him no tree of knowledge is forbid,
Or sweeter if forbid. How save the ark,
Or holy of holies, unprofaned a day
From his unscrupulous curiosity
That handles everything as if to buy,
Tossing aside what fabrics delicate

Suit not the rough-and-tumble of his ways?
What hope for those fine-nerved humanities
That made earth gracious once with gentler
arts,
Now the rude hands have caught the trick of
thought
And claim an equal suffrage with the brain?

The born disciple of an elder time,
(To me sufficient, friendlier than the new,)
Who in my blood feel motions of the Past,
I thank benignant Nature most for this, —
A force of sympathy, or call it lack
Of character firm-planted, loosing me
From the pent chamber of habitual self
To dwell enlarged in alien modes of thought,
Haply distasteful, wholesomer for that,
And through imagination to possess,

As they were mine, the lives of other men.
This growth original of virgin soil,
By fascination felt in opposites,
Pleases and shocks, entices and perturbs.
In this brown-fisted rough, this shirt-sleeved Cid,
This backwoods Charlemagne of empires new,
Whose blundering heel instinctively finds out
The goutier foot of speechless dignities,
Who, meeting Cæsar's self, would slap his back,
Call him "Old Horse," and challenge to a drink,
My lungs draw braver air, my breast dilates
With ampler manhood, and I front both worlds,
Of sense and spirit, as my natural fiefs,
To shape and then reshape them as I will.
It was the first man's charter; why not mine?
How forfeit? when deposed in other hands?

Thou shudder'st, Ovid? Dost in him forebode
A new avatar of the large-limbed Goth,
To break, or seem to break, tradition's clew,
And chase to dreamland back thy gods de-
throned?
I think man's soul dwells nearer to the east,
Nearer to morning's fountains than the sun;
Herself the source whence all tradition sprang,
Herself at once both labyrinth and clew.
The miracle fades out of history,
But faith and wonder and the primal earth
Are born into the world with every child.
Shall this self-maker with the prying eyes,
This creature disenchanted of respect
By the New World's new fiend, Publicity,
Whose testing thumb leaves everywhere its
smutch,
Not one day feel within himself the need

Of loyalty to better than himself,
That shall ennoble him with the upward look?
Shall he not catch the Voice that wanders earth,
With spiritual summons, dreamed or heard,
As sometimes, just ere sleep seals up the sense,
We hear our mother call from deeps of Time,
And, waking, find it vision, — none the less
The benediction bides, old skies return,
And that unreal thing, pre-eminent,
Makes air and dream of all we see and feel?
Shall he divine no strength unmade of votes,
Inward, impregnable, found soon as sought,
Not cognizable of sense, o'er sense supreme?
His holy places may not be of stone,
Nor made with hands, yet fairer far than aught
By artist feigned or pious ardor reared,
Fit altars for who guards inviolate

God's chosen seat, the sacred form of man.
Doubtless his church will be no hospital
For superannuate forms and mumping shams,
No parlor where men issue policies
Of life-assurance on the Eternal Mind,
Nor his religion but an ambulance
To fetch life's wounded and malingerers in,
Scorned by the strong; yet he, unconscious heir
To the influence sweet of Athens and of Rome,
And old Judæa's gift of secret fire,
Spite of himself shall surely learn to know
And worship some ideal of himself,
Some divine thing, large-hearted, brotherly,
Not nice in trifles, a soft creditor,
Pleased with his world, and hating only cant.
And, if his Church be doubtful, it is sure
That, in a world, made for whatever else,

Not made for mere enjoyment, in a world
Of toil but half-requited, or, at best,
Paid in some futile currency of breath,
A world of incompleteness, sorrow swift
And consolation laggard, whatsoe'er
The form of building or the creed professed,
The Cross, bold type of shame to homage turned,
Of an unfinished life that sways the world,
Shall tower as sovereign emblem over all.

The kobold Thought moves with us when we shift
Our dwelling to escape him; perched aloft
On the first load of household-stuff he went;
For, where the mind goes, goes old furniture.
I, who to Chartres came to feed my eye
And give to Fancy one clear holiday,

Scarce saw the minster for the thoughts it
stirred
Buzzing o'er past and future with vain quest.
Here once there stood a homely wooden
church,
Which slow devotion nobly changed for this
That echoes vaguely to my modern steps.
By suffrage universal it was built,
As practised then, for all the country came
From far as Rouen, to give votes for God,
Each vote a block of stone securely laid
Obedient to the master's deep-mused plan.
Will what our ballots rear, responsible
To no grave forethought, stand so long as this?
Delight like this the eye of after days
Brightening with pride that here, at least, were
men
Who meant and did the noblest thing they
knew?

Can our religion cope with deeds like this?
We, too, build Gothic contract-shams, because
Our deacons have discovered that it pays,
And pews sell better under vaulted roofs
Of plaster painted like an Indian squaw.
Shall not that Western Goth, of whom we spoke,
So fiercely practical, so keen of eye,
Find out, some day, that nothing pays but God,
Served whether on the smoke-shut battle-field,
In work obscure done honestly, or vote
For truth unpopular, or faith maintained
To ruinous convictions, or good deeds
Wrought for good's sake, mindless of heaven or hell?
Shall he not learn that all prosperity,
Whose bases stretch not deeper than the sense,
Is but a trick of this world's atmosphere,

A desert-born mirage of spire and dome,
Or find too late, the Past's long lesson missed,
That dust the prophets shake from off their feet
Grows heavy to drag down both tower and wall?
I know not; but, sustained by sure belief
That man still rises level with the height
Of noblest opportunities, or makes
Such, if the time supply not, I can wait.
I gaze round on the windows, pride of France,
Each the bright gift of some mechanic guild
Who loved their city and thought gold well
spent
To make her beautiful with piety;
I pause, transfigured by some stripe of bloom,
And my mind throngs with shining auguries,
Circle on circle, bright as seraphim,
With golden trumpets, silent, that await
The signal to blow news of good to men.

Then the revulsion came that always comes
After these dizzy elations of the mind:
And with a passionate pang of doubt I cried,
"O mountain-born, sweet with snow-filtered air
From uncontaminate wells of ether drawn
And never-broken secrecies of sky,
Freedom, with anguish won, misprized till lost,
They keep thee not who from thy sacred eyes
Catch the consuming lust of sensual good
And the brute's license of unfettered will.
Far from the popular shout and venal breath
Of Cleon blowing the mob's baser mind
To bubbles of wind-piloted conceit,
Thou shrinkest, gathering up thy skirts, to hide
In fortresses of solitary thought
And private virtue strong in self-restraint.
Must we too forfeit thee misunderstood,
Content with names, nor inly wise to know

That best things perish of their own excess,
And quality o'er-driven becomes defect?
Nay, is it thou indeed that we have glimpsed,
Or rather such illusion as of old
Through Athens glided menadlike and Rome,
A shape of vapor, mother of vain dreams
And mutinous traditions, specious plea
Of the glaived tyrant and long-memoried
priest?"

I walked forth saddened; for all thought is
sad,
And leaves a bitterish savor in the brain,
Tonic, it may be, not delectable,
And turned, reluctant, for a parting look
At those old weather-pitted images
Of bygone struggle, now so sternly calm.
About their shoulders sparrows had built nests,

And fluttered, chirping, from gray perch to
perch,
Now on a mitre poising, now a crown,
Irreverently happy. While I thought
How confident they were, what careless hearts
Flew on those lightsome wings and shared the
sun,
A larger shadow crossed; and looking up,
I saw where, nesting in the hoary towers,
The sparrow-hawk slid forth on noiseless air,
With sidelong head that watched the joy below,
Grim Norman baron o'er this clan of Kelts.
Enduring Nature, force conservative,
Indifferent to our noisy whims! Men prate
Of all heads to an equal grade cashiered
On level with the dullest, and expect
(Sick of no worse distemper than themselves)
A wondrous cure-all in equality;

They reason that To-morrow must be wise
Because To-day was not, nor Yesterday,
As if good days were shapen of themselves,
Not of the very lifeblood of men's souls;
Meanwhile, long-suffering, imperturbable,
Thou quietly complet'st thy syllogism,
And from the premise sparrow here below
Draw'st sure conclusion of the hawk above,
Pleased with the soft-billed songster, pleased
no less
With the fierce beak of natures aquiline.

Thou beautiful Old Time, now hid away
In the Past's valley of Avilion,
Haply, like Arthur, till thy wound be healed,
Then to reclaim the sword and crown again!
Thrice beautiful to us; perchance less fair
To who possessed thee, as a mountain seems

To dwellers round its bases but a heap
Of barren obstacle that lairs the storm
And the avalanche's silent bolt holds back
Leashed with a hair, — meanwhile some far-off clown,
Hereditary delver of the plain,
Sees it an unmoved vision of repose,
Nest of the morning, and conjectures there
The dance of streams to idle shepherds' pipes,
And fairer habitations softly hung
On breezy slopes, or hid in valleys cool,
For happier men. No mortal ever dreams
That the scant isthmus he encamps upon
Between two oceans, one, the Stormy, passed,
And one, the Peaceful, yet to venture on,
Has been that future whereto prophets yearned
For the fulfilment of Earth's cheated hope,
Shall be that past which nerveless poets moan

As the lost opportunity of song.
O Power, more near my life than life itself
(Or what seems life to us in sense immured),
Even as the roots, shut in the darksome earth,
Share in the tree-top's joyance, and conceive
Of sunshine and wide air and wingëd things
By sympathy of nature, so do I
Have evidence of Thee so far above,
Yet in and of me! Rather Thou the root
Invisibly sustaining, hid in light,
Not darkness, or in darkness made by us.
If sometimes I must hear good men debate
Of other witness of Thyself than Thou,
As if there needed any help of ours
To nurse Thy flickering life, that else must cease,
Blown out, as 't were a candle, by men's breath,
My soul shall not be taken in their snare,

To change her inward surety for their doubt
Muffled from sight in formal robes of proof:
While she can only feel herself through Thee,
I fear not Thy withdrawal; more I fear,
Seeing, to know Thee not, hoodwinked with dreams
Of signs and wonders, while, unnoticed, Thou,
Walking Thy garden still, commun'st with men,
Missed in the commonplace of miracle.

ODE

RECITED AT THE HARVARD COMMEMORATION,
JULY 21, 1865.

ODE.

I.

EAK-WINGED is song,
Nor aims at that clear-ethered height
Whither the brave deed climbs for light:
We seem to do them wrong,
Bringing our robin's-leaf to deck their hearse
Who in warm life-blood wrote their nobler verse,
Our trivial song to honor those who come
With ears attuned to strenuous trump and drum,

And shaped in squadron-strophes their desire,
Live battle-odes whose lines were steel and
fire:
Yet sometimes feathered words are strong,
A gracious memory to buoy up and save
From Lethe's dreamless ooze, the common
grave
Of the unventurous throng.

II.

To-day our Reverend Mother welcomes back
Her wisest Scholars, those who understood
The deeper teaching of her mystic tome,
And offered their fresh lives to make it good:
No lore of Greece or Rome,
No science peddling with the names of things,
Or reading stars to find inglorious fates,
Can lift our life with wings

Far from Death's idle gulf that for the many
waits,
And lengthen out our dates
With that clear fame whose memory sings
In manly hearts to come, and nerves them and
dilates:
Nor such thy teaching, Mother of us all!
Not such the trumpet-call
Of thy diviner mood,
That could thy sons entice
From happy homes and toils, the fruitful
nest
Of those half-virtues which the world calls
best,
Into War's tumult rude;
But rather far that stern device
The sponsors chose that round thy cradle stood
In the dim, unventured wood,

The VERITAS that lurks beneath
The letter's unprolific sheath,
Life of whate'er makes life worth living,
Seed-grain of high emprise, immortal food,
One heavenly thing whereof earth hath the giving.

III.

Many loved Truth, and lavished life's best oil
Amid the dust of books to find her,
Content at last, for guerdon of their toil,
With the cast mantle she hath left behind her.
Many in sad faith sought for her,
Many with crossed hands sighed for her;
But these, our brothers, fought for her,
At life's dear peril wrought for her,
So loved her that they died for her,

Tasting the raptured fleetness
Of her divine completeness:
Their higher instinct knew
Those love her best who to themselves are true,
And what they dare to dream of, dare to do;
They followed her and found her
Where all may hope to find,
Not in the ashes of the burnt-out mind,
But beautiful, with danger's sweetness round her.
Where faith made whole with deed
Breathes its awakening breath
Into the lifeless creed,
They saw her plumed and mailed,
With sweet, stern face unveiled,
And all-repaying eyes, look proud on them in death.

IV.

Our slender life runs rippling by, and glides
Into the silent hollow of the past;
What is there that abides
To make the next age better for the last?
Is earth too poor to give us
Something to live for here that shall outlive
us?
Some more substantial boon
Than such as flows and ebbs with Fortune's
fickle moon?
The little that we see
From doubt is never free;
The little that we do
Is but half-nobly true;
With our laborious hiving
What men call treasure, and the gods call dross,

Life seems a jest of Fate's contriving,
Only secure in every one's conniving,
A long account of nothings paid with loss,
Where we poor puppets, jerked by unseen wires,
After our little hour of strut and rave,
With all our pasteboard passions and desires,
Loves, hates, ambitions, and immortal fires,
Are tossed pell-mell together in the grave.
But stay! no age was e'er degenerate,
Unless men held it at too cheap a rate,
For in our likeness still we shape our fate.
Ah, there is something here
Unfathomed by the cynic's sneer,
Something that gives our feeble light
A high immunity from Night,
Something that leaps life's narrow bars
To claim its birthright with the hosts of heaven;

A seed of sunshine that doth leaven
Our earthly dulness with the beams of stars,
And glorify our clay
With light from fountains elder than the Day;
A conscience more divine than we,
A gladness fed with secret tears,
A vexing, forward-reaching sense
Of some more noble permanence;
A light across the sea,
Which haunts the soul and will not let it be,
Still glimmering from the heights of undegenerate years.

V.

Whither leads the path
To ampler fates that leads?
Not down through flowery meads,

To reap an aftermath
Of youth's vainglorious weeds,
But up the steep, amid the wrath
And shock of deadly-hostile creeds,
Where the world's best hope and stay
By battle's flashes gropes a desperate way,
And every turf the fierce foot clings to bleeds.
Peace hath her not ignoble wreath,
Ere yet the sharp, decisive word
Light the black lips of cannon, and the sword
Dreams in its easeful sheath;
But some day the live coal behind the thought,
Whether from Baäl's stone obscene,
Or from the shrine serene
Of God's pure altar brought,
Bursts up in flame; the war of tongue and pen
Learns with what deadly purpose it was fraught,
And, helpless in the fiery passion caught,

Shakes all the pillared state with shock of men:
Some day the soft Ideal that we wooed
Confronts us fiercely, foe-beset, pursued,
And cries reproachful: "Was it, then, my
praise,
And not myself was loved? Prove now thy
truth;
I claim of thee the promise of thy youth;
Give me thy life, or cower in empty phrase,
The victim of thy genius, not its mate!"
Life may be given in many ways,
And loyalty to Truth be sealed
As bravely in the closet as the field,
So bountiful is Fate;
But then to stand beside her,
When craven churls deride her,
To front a lie in arms and not to yield,
This shows, methinks, God's plan

And measure of a stalwart man,
Limbed like the old heroic breeds,
Who stands self-poised on manhood's solid earth,
Not forced to frame excuses for his birth,
Fed from within with all the strength he needs.

VI.

Such was he, our Martyr-Chief,
Whom late the Nation he had led,
With ashes on her head,
Wept with the passion of an angry grief:
Forgive me, if from present things I turn
To speak what in my heart will beat and burn,
And hang my wreath on his world-honored urn.
Nature, they say, doth dote,
And cannot make a man

Save on some worn-out plan,
Repeating us by rote:
For him her Old-World moulds aside she threw,
And, choosing sweet clay from the breast
Of the unexhausted West,
With stuff untainted shaped a hero new,
Wise, steadfast in the strength of God, and true.
How beautiful to see
Once more a shepherd of mankind indeed,
Who loved his charge, but never loved to lead;
One whose meek flock the people joyed to be,
Not lured by any cheat of birth,
But by his clear-grained human worth,
And brave old wisdom of sincerity!
They knew that outward grace is dust;
They could not choose but trust
In that sure-footed mind's unfaltering skill,
And supple-tempered will

That bent like perfect steel to spring again and
thrust.
His was no lonely mountain-peak of mind,
Thrusting to thin air o'er our cloudy bars,
A sea-mark now, now lost in vapors blind;
Broad prairie rather, genial, level-lined,
Fruitful and friendly for all human kind,
Yet also nigh to heaven and loved of loftiest
stars.
Nothing of Europe here,
Or, then, of Europe fronting mornward still,
Ere any names of Serf and Peer
Could Nature's equal scheme deface
And thwart her genial will;
Here was a type of the true elder race,
And one of Plutarch's men talked with us face
to face.
I praise him not; it were too late;

And some innative weakness there must be
In him who condescends to victory
Such as the Present gives, and cannot wait,
Safe in himself as in a fate.
So always firmly he:
He knew to bide his time,
And can his fame abide,
Still patient in his simple faith sublime,
Till the wise years decide.
Great captains, with their guns and drums,
Disturb our judgment for the hour,
But at last silence comes;
These all are gone, and, standing like a
tower,
Our children shall behold his fame,
The kindly-earnest, brave, foreseeing man,
Sagacious, patient, dreading praise, not blame,
New birth of our new soil, the first American.

VII.

Long as man's hope insatiate can discern
Or only guess some more inspiring goal
Outside of Self, enduring as the pole,
Along whose course the flying axles burn
Of spirits bravely-pitched, earth's manlier brood;
Long as below we cannot find
The meed that stills the inexorable mind;
So long this faith to some ideal Good,
Under whatever mortal names it masks,
Freedom, Law, Country, this ethereal mood
That thanks the Fates for their severer tasks,
Feeling its challenged pulses leap,
While others skulk in subterfuges cheap,
And, set in Danger's van, has all the boon it asks,

Shall win man's praise and woman's love,
Shall be a wisdom that we set above
All other skills and gifts to culture dear,
A virtue round whose forehead we inwreathe
Laurels that with a living passion breathe
When other crowns grow, while we twine them,
sear.
What brings us thronging these high rites
to pay,
And seal these hours the noblest of our year,
Save that our brothers found this better
way?

VIII.

We sit here in the Promised Land
That flows with Freedom's honey and milk;
But 't was they won it, sword in hand,
Making the nettle danger soft for us as silk

We welcome back our bravest and our
best; —
Ah me! not all! some come not with the
rest,
Who went forth brave and bright as any here!
I strive to mix some gladness with my strain,
But the sad strings complain,
And will not please the ear:
I sweep them for a pæan, but they wane
Again and yet again
Into a dirge, and die away, in pain.
In these brave ranks I only see the gaps,
Thinking of dear ones whom the dumb turf
wraps,
Dark to the triumph which they died to
gain:
Fitlier may others greet the living,
For me the past is unforgiving;

I with uncovered head
Salute the sacred dead,
Who went, and who return not. — Say not so!
'T is not the grapes of Canaan that repay,
But the high faith that failed not by the way;
Virtue treads paths that end not in the grave;
No bar of endless night exiles the brave;
And to the saner mind
We rather seem the dead that stayed behind.
Blow, trumpets, all your exultations blow!
For never shall their aureoled presence lack:
I see them muster in a gleaming row,
With ever-youthful brows that nobler show;
We find in our dull road their shining track;
In every nobler mood
We feel the orient of their spirit glow,
Part of our life's unalterable good,

Of all our saintlier aspiration ;
They come transfigured back,
Secure from change in their high-hearted ways
Beautiful evermore, and with the rays
Of morn on their white Shields of Expectation !

IX.

But is there hope to save
Even this ethereal essence from the grave ?
What ever 'scaped Oblivion's subtle wrong
Save a few clarion names, or golden threads
of song ?
Before my musing eye
The mighty ones of old sweep by,
Disvoicëd now and insubstantial things,
As noisy once as we ; poor ghosts of kings,
Shadows of empire wholly gone to dust,
And many races, nameless long ago,

To darkness driven by that imperious gust
Of ever-rushing Time that here doth blow:
O visionary world, condition strange,
Where naught abiding is but only Change,
Where the deep-bolted stars themselves still shift and range!
Shall we to more continuance make pretence?
Renown builds tombs; a life-estate is Wit;
And, bit by bit,
The cunning years steal all from us but woe;
Leaves are we, whose decays no harvest sow.
But, when we vanish hence,
Shall they lie forceless in the dark below,
Save to make green their little length of sods,
Or deepen pansies for a year or two,

Who now to us are shining-sweet as gods?
Was dying all they had the skill to do?
That were not fruitless: but the Soul resents
Such short-lived service, as if blind events
Ruled without her, or earth could so endure;
She claims a more divine investiture
Of longer tenure than Fame's airy rents;
Whate'er she touches doth her nature share;
Her inspiration haunts the ennobled air,
Gives eyes to mountains blind,
Ears to the deaf earth, voices to the wind,
And her clear trump sings succor everywhere
By lonely bivouacs to the wakeful mind;
For soul inherits all that soul could dare:
Yea, Manhood hath a wider span
And larger privilege of life than man.

The single deed, the private sacrifice,
So radiant now through proudly-hidden tears,
Is covered up erelong from mortal eyes
With thoughtless drift of the deciduous years;
But that high privilege that makes all men peers,
That leap of heart whereby a people rise
Up to a noble anger's height,
And, flamed on by the Fates, not shrink, but grow more bright,
That swift validity in noble veins,
Of choosing danger and disdaining shame,
Of being set on flame
By the pure fire that flies all contact base,
But wraps its chosen with angelic might,
These are imperishable gains,

Sure as the sun, medicinal as light,
These hold great futures in their lusty reins
And certify to earth a new imperial race.

X.

Who now shall sneer?
Who dare again to say we trace
Our lines to a plebeian race?
Roundhead and Cavalier!
Dumb are those names erewhile in battle loud;
Dream-footed as the shadow of a cloud,
They flit across the ear:
That is best blood that hath most iron in 't.
To edge resolve with, pouring without stint
For what makes manhood dear.
Tell us not of Plantagenets,
Hapsburgs, and Guelfs, whose thin bloods crawl

Down from some victor in a border-brawl!
How poor their outworn coronets,
Matched with one leaf of that plain civic wreath
Our brave for honor's blazon shall bequeath,
Through whose desert a rescued Nation sets
Her heel on treason, and the trumpet hears
Shout victory, tingling Europe's sullen ears
With vain resentments and more vain regrets!

XI.

Not in anger, not in pride,
Pure from passion's mixture rude
Ever to base earth allied,
But with far-heard gratitude,
Still with heart and voice renewed,
To heroes living and dear martyrs dead,

The strain should close that consecrates our brave.
Lift the heart and lift the head!
Lofty be its mood and grave,
Not without a martial ring,
Not without a prouder tread
And a peal of exultation:
Little right has he to sing
Through whose heart in such an hour
Beats no march of conscious power,
Sweeps no tumult of elation!
'T is no Man we celebrate,
By his country's victories great,
A hero half, and half the whim of Fate,
But the pith and marrow of a Nation
Drawing force from all her men,
Highest, humblest, weakest, all,
For her time of need, and then

Pulsing it again through them,
Till the basest can no longer cower,
Feeling his soul spring up divinely tall,
Touched but in passing by her mantle-hem.
Come back, then, noble pride, for 't is her dower!
How could poet ever tower,
If his passions, hopes, and fears,
If his triumphs and his tears,
Kept not measure with his people?
Boom, cannon, boom to all the winds and waves!
Clash out, glad bells, from every rocking steeple!
Banners, advance with triumph, bend your staves!
And from every mountain-peak
Let beacon-fire to answering beacon speak,

Katahdin tell Monadnock, Whiteface he,
And so leap on in light from sea to sea,
Till the glad news be sent
Across a kindling continent,
Making earth feel more firm and air breathe braver:
"Be proud! for she is saved, and all have helped to save her!
She that lifts up the manhood of the poor,
She of the open soul and open door,
With room about her hearth for all mankind!
The fire is dreadful in her eyes no more;
From her bold front the helm she doth unbind,
Sends all her handmaid armies back to spin,
And bids her navies, that so lately hurled

Their crashing battle, hold their thunders
in,
Swimming like birds of calm along the unharmful shore.
No challenge sends she to the elder world,
That looked askance and hated; a light
scorn
Plays o'er her mouth, as round her mighty
knees
She calls her children back, and waits the
morn
Of nobler day, enthroned between her subject
seas."

XII.

Bow down, dear Land, for thou hast found release!
Thy God, in these distempered days,

Hath taught thee the sure wisdom of His
ways,
And through thine enemies hath wrought thy
peace!
Bow down in prayer and praise!
No poorest in thy borders but may now
Lift to the juster skies a man's enfranchised
brow,
O Beautiful! my Country! ours once more!
Smoothing thy gold of war-dishevelled hair
O'er such sweet brows as never other wore,
And letting thy set lips,
Freed from wrath's pale eclipse,
The rosy edges of their smile lay bare,
What words divine of lover or of poet
Could tell our love and make thee know it,
Among the Nations bright beyond compare?
What were our lives without thee?

What all our lives to save thee?
We reck not what we gave thee;
We will not dare to doubt thee,
But ask whatever else, and we will dare!

FAVORITE POEMS.

FAVORITE POEMS.

CONTENTS.

ILLUSTRATIONS.

MY LOVE.

OT as all other women are
Is she that to my soul is dear ;
Her glorious fancies come from far,
Beneath the silver evening-star,
And yet her heart is ever near.

Great feelings hath she of her own,
Which lesser souls may never know ;
God giveth them to her alone,
And sweet they are as any tone
Wherewith the wind may choose to blow.

Yet in herself she dwelleth not,
Although no home were half so fair ;
No simplest duty is forgot,
Life hath no dim and lowly spot
That doth not in her sunshine share.
She doeth little kindnesses,

Which most leave undone, or despise :
For naught that sets one heart at ease,
And giveth happiness or peace,
Is low-esteemëd in her eyes.

She hath no scorn of common things,
And, though she seem of other birth,
Round us her heart intwines and clings,
And patiently she folds her wings
To tread the humble paths of earth.

Blessing she is : God made her so,
And deeds of week-day holiness
Fall from her noiseless as the snow,
Nor hath she ever chanced to know
That aught were easier than to bless.

She is most fair, and thereunto
Her life doth rightly harmonize ;
Feeling or thought that was not true
Ne'er made less beautiful the blue
Unclouded heaven of her eyes.

She is a woman : one in whom
The spring-time of her childish years
Hath never lost its fresh perfume,

Though knowing well that life hath room
For many blights and many tears.

I love her with a love as still
As a broad river's peaceful might,
Which, by high tower and lowly mill,
Goes wandering at its own will,
And yet doth ever flow aright.

And, on its full, deep breast serene,
Like quiet isles my duties lie ;
It flows around them and between,
And makes them fresh and fair and green,
Sweet homes wherein to live and die.

ABOVE AND BELOW.

I.

DWELLERS in the valley-land,
Who in deep twilight grope and cower,
Till the slow mountain's dial-hand
Shortens to noon's triumphal hour,

While ye sit idle, do ye think
  The Lord's great work sits idle too?
That light dare not o'erleap the brink
  Of morn, because 't is dark with you?

Though yet your valleys skulk in night,
  In God's ripe fields the day is cried,
And reapers, with their sickles bright,
  Troop, singing, down the mountain-side:
Come up, and feel what health there is
  In the frank Dawn's delighted eyes,
As, bending with a pitying kiss,
  The night-shed tears of Earth she dries!

The Lord wants reapers: O, mount up,
  Before night comes, and says, "Too late!"
Stay not for taking scrip or cup,
  The Master hungers while ye wait;
'T is from these heights alone your eyes
  The advancing spears of day can see,
That o'er the eastern hill-tops rise,
  To break your long captivity.

II.

Lone watcher on the mountain-height,
  It is right precious to behold

The first long surf of climbing light
  Flood all the thirsty east with gold ;
But we, who in the shadow sit,
  Know also when the day is nigh,
Seeing thy shining forehead lit
  With his inspiring prophecy.

Thou hast thine office ; we have ours ;
  God lacks not early service here,
But what are thine eleventh hours
  He counts with us for morning cheer ;
Our day, for Him, is long enough,
  And when he giveth work to do,
The bruisëd reed is amply tough
  To pierce the shield of error through.

But not the less do thou aspire
  Light's earlier messages to preach ;
Keep back no syllable of fire,
  Plunge deep the rowels of thy speech.
Yet God deems not thine aeried sight
  More worthy than our twilight dim ;
For meek Obedience, too, is Light,
  And following that is finding Him.

THE CHANGELING.

 HAD a little daughter,
And she was given to me
To lead me gently backward
To the Heavenly Father's knee,
That I, by the force of nature,
Might in some dim wise divine
The depth of his infinite patience
To this wayward soul of mine.

I know not how others saw her,
But to me she was wholly fair,
And the light of the heaven she came from
Still lingered and gleamed in her hair;
For it was as wavy and golden,
And as many changes took,
As the shadows of sun-gilt ripples
On the yellow bed of a brook.

To what can I liken her smiling
Upon me, her kneeling lover,
How it leaped from her lips to her eyelids,
And dimpled her wholly over,

Till her outstretched hands smiled also,
  And I almost seemed to see
The very heart of her mother
  Sending sun through her veins to me !

She had been with us scarce a twelvemonth,
  And it hardly seemed a day,
When a troop of wandering angels
  Stole my little daughter away ;
Or perhaps those heavenly Zingari
  But loosed the hampering strings,
And when they had opened her cage-door,
  My little bird used her wings.

But they left instead a changeling,
  A little angel child,
That seems like her bud in full blossom,
  And smiles as she never smiled :
When I wake in the morning, I see it
  Where she always used to lie,
And I feel as weak as a violet
  Alone 'neath the awful sky.

As weak, yet as trustful also ;
  For the whole year long I see

All the wonders of faithful Nature
  Still worked for the love of me ;
Winds wander, and dews drip earthward,
  Rain falls, suns rise and set,
Earth whirls, and all but to prosper
  A poor little violet.

This child is not mine as the first was,
  I cannot sing it to rest,
I cannot lift it up fatherly
  And bliss it upon my breast ;
Yet it lies in my little one's cradle
  And sits in my little one's chair,
And the light of the heaven she 's gone to
  Transfigures its golden hair.

THE SHEPHERD OF KING ADMETUS.

THERE came a youth upon the earth,
  Some thousand years ago,
Whose slender hands were nothing worth,
Whether to plough, or reap, or sow.

Upon an empty tortoise-shell
  He stretched some chords, and drew
Music that made men's bosoms swell
Fearless, or brimmed their eyes with dew.

Then King Admetus, one who had
  Pure taste by right divine,
Decreed his singing not too bad
To hear between the cups of wine :

And so, well pleased with being soothed
  Into a sweet half-sleep,
Three times his kingly beard he smoothed,
And made him viceroy o'er his sheep.

His words were simple words enough,
  And yet he used them so,
That what in other mouths was rough
In his seemed musical and low.

Men called him but a shiftless youth,
  In whom no good they saw ;
And yet, unwittingly, in truth,
They made his careless words their law.

They knew not how he learned at all,
For idly, hour by hour,
He sat and watched the dead leaves fall,
Or mused upon a common flower.

It seemed the loveliness of things
Did teach him all their use,
For, in mere weeds, and stones, and springs,
He found a healing power profuse.

Men granted that his speech was wise,
But, when a glance they caught
Of his slim grace and woman's eyes,
They laughed, and called him good-for-naught.

Yet after he was dead and gone,
And e'en his memory dim,
Earth seemed more sweet to live upon,
More full of love, because of him.

And day by day more holy grew
Each spot where he had trod,
Till after-poets only knew
Their first-born brother as a god.

AMBROSE.

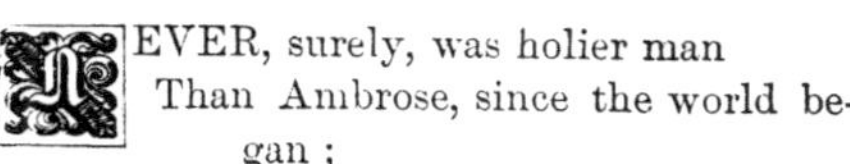EVER, surely, was holier man
Than Ambrose, since the world be-
gan ;
With diet spare and raiment thin
He shielded himself from the father of sin ;
With bed of iron and scourgings oft,
His heart to God's hand as wax made soft.

Through earnest prayer and watchings long
He sought to know 'tween right and wrong,
Much wrestling with the blessed Word
To make it yield the sense of the Lord,
That he might build a storm-proof creed
To fold the flock in at their need.

At last he builded a perfect faith,
Fenced round about with *The Lord thus saith ;*
To himself he fitted the doorway's size,
Meted the light to the need of his eyes,
And knew, by a sure and inward sign,
That the work of his fingers was divine.

Then Ambrose said, "All those shall die
The eternal death who believe not as I";
And some were boiled, some burned in fire,
Some sawn in twain, that his heart's desire,
For the good of men's souls, might be satisfied
By the drawing of all to the righteous side.

One day, as Ambrose was seeking the truth
In his lonely walk, he saw a youth
Resting himself in the shade of a tree;
It had never been granted him to see
So shining a face, and the good man thought
'T were pity he should not believe as he ought.

So he set himself by the young man's side,
And the state of his soul with questions tried;
But the heart of the stranger was hardened indeed,
Nor received the stamp of the one true creed;
And the spirit of Ambrose waxed sore to find
Such face the porch of so narrow a mind.

"As each beholds in cloud and fire
The shape that answers his own desire,
So each," said the youth, "in the Law shall
find
The figure and features of his mind;
And to each in his mercy hath God allowed
His several pillar of fire and cloud."

The soul of Ambrose burned with zeal
And holy wrath for the young man's weal:
"Believest thou then, most wretched youth,"
Cried he, "a dividual essence in Truth?
I fear me thy heart is too cramped with sin
To take the Lord in his glory in."

Now there bubbled beside them where they
stood
A fountain of waters sweet and good;
The youth to the streamlet's brink drew near
Saying, "Ambrose, thou maker of creeds,
look here!"
Six vases of crystal then he took,
And set them along the edge of the brook.

"As into these vessels the water I pour,
There shall one hold less, another more,

And the water unchanged, in every case,
Shall put on the figure of the vase ;
O thou, who wouldst unity make through strife,
Canst thou fit this sign to the Water of Life ?"

When Ambrose looked up, he stood alone,
The youth and the stream and the vases were gone ;
But he knew, by a sense of humbled grace,
He had talked with an angel face to face,
And felt his heart change inwardly,
As he fell on his knees beneath the tree.

MASACCIO.

IN THE BRANCACCI CHAPEL.

HE came to Florence long ago,
And painted here these walls, that shone
For Raphael and for Angelo,
With secrets deeper than his own,
Then shrank into the dark again,
And died, we know not how or when.

The shadows deepened, and I turned
Half sadly from the fresco grand ;
"And is this," mused I, "all ye earned,
High-vaulted brain and cunning hand,
That ye to greater men could teach
The skill yourselves could never reach ?"

"And who were they," I mused, "that wrought
Through pathless wilds, with labor long,
The highways of our daily thought ?
Who reared those towers of earliest song
That lift us from the throng to peace
Remote in sunny silences ?"

Out clanged the Ave Mary bells,
And to my heart this message came :
Each clamorous throat among them tells
What strong-souled martyrs died in flame
To make it possible that thou
Shouldst here with brother-sinners bow.

Thoughts that great hearts once broke for, we
Breathe cheaply in the common air ;
The dust we trample heedlessly

Throbbed once in saints and heroes rare,
Who perished, opening for their race
New pathways to the commonplace.

Henceforth, when rings the health to those
Who live in story and in song,
O nameless dead, that now repose
Safe in Oblivion's chambers strong,
One cup of recognition true
Shall silently be drained to you!

AN INCIDENT OF THE FIRE AT HAMBURG.

THE tower of old Saint Nicholas soared upward to the skies,
Like some huge piece of Nature's make, the growth of centuries;
You could not deem its crowding spires a work of human art,
They seemed to struggle lightward from a sturdy living heart.

Not Nature's self more freely speaks in crystal or in oak,

Than through the pious builder's hand, in
that gray pile she spoke;
And as from acorn springs the oak, so, freely
and alone,
Sprang from his heart this hymn to God,
sung in obedient stone.

It seemed a wondrous freak of chance, so perfect, yet so rough,
A whim of Nature crystallized slowly in
granite tough;
The thick spires yearned towards the sky in
quaint harmonious lines,
And in broad sunlight basked and slept, like
a grove of blasted pines.

Never did rock or stream or tree lay claim
with better right
To all the adorning sympathies of shadow
and of light;
And in that forest petrified as forester, there
dwells
Stout Herman, the old sacristan, sole lord of
all its bells.

Surge leaping after surge, the fire roared onward red as blood,
Till half of Hamburg lay engulfed beneath the eddying flood;
For miles away the fiery spray poured down its deadly rain,
And back and forth the billows sucked, and paused, and burst again.

From square to square with tiger leaps panted the lustful fire,
The air to leeward shuddered with the gasps of its desire;
And church and palace, which even now stood whelmed but to the knee,
Lift their black roofs like breakers lone amid the whirling sea.

Up in his tower old Herman sat and watched with quiet look;
His soul had trusted God too long to be at last forsook;
He could not fear, for surely God a pathway would unfold
Through this red sea for faithful hearts, as once he did of old.

But scarcely can he cross himself, or on his
good saint call,
Before the sacrilegious flood o'erleaped the
churchyard wall;
And, ere a pater half was said, mid smoke
and crackling glare,
His island tower scarce juts its head above
the wide despair.

Upon the peril's desperate peak his heart
stood up sublime;
His first thought was for God above, his next
was for his chime;
"Sing now and make your voices heard in
hymns of praise," cried he,
"As did the Israelites of old, safe walking
through the sea!

"Through this red sea our God hath made a
pathway safe to shore;
Our promised land stands full in sight; shout
now as ne'er before!"
And as the tower came crushing down, the
bells, in clear accord,
Pealed forth the grand old German hymn, —
"All good souls, praise the Lord!"

TO THE DANDELION.

EAR common flower, that grow'st beside the way,
Fringing the dusty road with harmless gold,
First pledge of blithesome May,
Which children pluck, and, full of pride uphold,
High-hearted buccaneers, o'erjoyed that they
An Eldorado in the grass have found,
Which not the rich earth's ample round
May match in wealth, thou art more dear to me
Than all the prouder summer-blooms may be.

Gold such as thine ne'er drew the Spanish prow
Through the primeval hush of Indian seas,
Nor wrinkled the lean brow
Of age, to rob the lover's heart of ease;
'T is the Spring's largess, which she scatters now

To rich and poor alike, with lavish hand,
Though most hearts never understand
To take it at God's value, but pass by
The offered wealth with unrewarded eye.

Thou art my tropics and mine Italy ;
To look at thee unlocks a warmer clime ;
The eyes thou givest me
Are in the heart, and heed not space or
time :
Not in mid June the golden-cuirassed
bee
Feels a more summer-like warm ravishment
In the white lily's breezy tent,
His fragrant Sybaris, than I, when first
From the dark green thy yellow circles
burst.

Then think I of deep shadows on the grass,
Of meadows where in sun the cattle graze,
Where, as the breezes pass,
The gleaming rushes lean a thousand ways,
Of leaves that slumber in a cloudy mass,
Or whiten in the wind, of waters blue
That from the distance sparkle through

Some woodland gap, and of a sky above,
Where one white cloud like a stray lamb doth move.

My childhood's earliest thoughts are linked with thee;
The sight of thee calls back the robin's song,
Who, from the dark old tree
Beside the door, sang clearly all day long,
And I, secure in childish piety,
Listened as if I heard an angel sing
With news from heaven, which he could bring
Fresh every day to my untainted ears
When birds and flowers and I were happy peers.

How like a prodigal doth nature seem,
When thou, for all thy gold, so common art!
Thou teachest me to deem
More sacredly of every human heart,
Since each reflects in joy its scanty gleam
Of heaven, and could some wondrous secret show,

Did we but pay the love we owe,
And with a child's undoubting wisdom
look
On all these living pages of God's book.

BEAVER BROOK.

HUSHED with broad sunlight lies the
hill,
And, minuting the long day's loss,
The cedar's shadow, slow and still,
Creeps o'er its dial of gray moss.

Warm noon brims full the valley's cup,
The aspen's leaves are scarce astir;
Only the little mill sends up
Its busy, never-ceasing burr.

Climbing the loose-piled wall that hems
The road along the mill-pond's brink,
From 'neath the arching barberry-stems,
My footstep scares the shy chewink.

Beneath a bony buttonwood
The mill's red door lets forth the din;

The whitened miller, dust-imbued,
Flits past the square of dark within.

No mountain torrent's strength is here;
Sweet Beaver, child of forest still,
Heaps its small pitcher to the ear,
And gently waits the miller's will.

Swift slips Undine along the race
Unheard, and then, with flashing bound,
Floods the dull wheel with light and grace,
And, laughing, hunts the loath drudge round.

The miller dreams not at what cost
The quivering millstones hum and whirl,
Nor how for every turn are tost
Armfuls of diamond and of pearl.

But Summer cleared my happier eyes
With drops of some celestial juice,
To see how Beauty underlies,
Forevermore each form of use.

And more; methought I saw that flood,
Which now so dull and darkling steals,
Thick, here and there, with human blood,
To turn the world's laborious wheels.

"Sweet beaver, child of forest still."

No more than doth the miller there,
Shut in our several cells, do we
Know with what waste of beauty rare
Moves every day's machinery.

Surely the wiser time shall come
When this fine overplus of might,
No longer sullen, slow, and dumb,
Shall leap to music and to light.

In that new childhood of the Earth
Life of itself shall dance and play,
Fresh blood in Time's shrunk veins make
mirth,
And labor meet delight half-way.

AN INTERVIEW WITH MILES STANDISH.

SAT one evening in my room,
In that sweet hour of twilight
When blended thoughts, half light,
half gloom,
Throng through the spirit's skylight ;

The flames by fits curled round the bars,
  Or up the chimney crinkled,
While embers dropped like falling stars,
  And in the ashes tinkled.

I sat and mused ; the fire burned low,
  And, o'er my senses stealing,
Crept something of the ruddy glow
  That bloomed on wall and ceiling ;
My pictures (they are very few,
  The heads of ancient wise men)
Smoothed down their knotted fronts, and grew
  As rosy as excisemen.

My antique high-backed Spanish chair
  Felt thrills through wood and leather,
That had been strangers since whilere,
  Mid Andalusian heather,
The oak that made its sturdy frame
  His happy arms stretched over
The ox whose fortunate hide became
  The bottom's polished cover.

It came out in that famous bark,
  That brought our sires intrepid,

Capacious as another ark
  For furniture decrepit ;
For, as that saved of bird and beast
  A pair for propagation,
So has the seed of these increased
  And furnished half the nation.

Kings sit, they say, in slippery seats ;
  But those slant precipices
Of ice the northern voyager meets
  Less slippery are than this is ;
To cling therein would pass the wit
  Of royal man or woman,
And whatsoe'er can stay in it
  Is more or less than human.

I offer to all bores this perch,
  Dear well-intentioned people
With heads as void as week-day church,
  Tongues longer than the steeple ;
To folks with missions, whose gaunt eyes
  See golden ages rising, —
Salt of the earth ! in what queer Guys
  Thou 'rt fond of crystallizing !

My wonder, then, was not unmixed
 With merciful suggestion,
When, as my roving eyes grew fixed
 Upon the chair in question,
I saw its trembling arms enclose
 A figure grim and rusty,
Whose doublet plain and plainer hose
 Were something worn and dusty.

Now even such men as Nature forms
 Merely to fill the street with,
Once turned to ghosts by hungry worms,
 Are serious things to meet with ;
Your penitent spirits are no jokes,
 And, though I 'm not averse to
A quiet shade, even they are folks
 One cares not to speak first to.

Who knows, thought I, but he has come,
 By Charon kindly ferried,
To tell me of a mighty sum
 Behind my wainscot buried ?
There is a buccaneerish air
 About that garb outlandish —
Just then the ghost drew up his chair
 And said, " My name is Standish.

"I come from Plymouth, deadly bored
With toasts, and songs, and speeches,
As long and flat as my old sword,
As threadbare as my breeches:
They understand us Pilgrims! they,
Smooth men with rosy faces,
Strength's knots and gnarls all pared away,
And varnish in their places!

"We had some toughness in our grain,
The eye to rightly see us is
Not just the one that lights the brain
Of drawing-room Tyrtæuses:
They talk about their Pilgrim blood,
Their birthright high and holy!
A mountain-stream that ends in mud
Methinks is melancholy.

"He had stiff knees, the Puritan,
That were not good at bending;
The homespun dignity of man
He thought was worth defending;
He did not, with his pinchbeck ore,
His country's shame forgotten,
Gild Freedom's coffin o'er and o'er,
When all within was rotten.

"These loud ancestral boasts of yours,
  How can they else than vex us?
Where were your dinner orators
  When slavery grasped at Texas?
Dumb on his knees was every one
  That now is bold as Cæsar;
Mere pegs to hang an office on
  Such stalwart men as these are."

"Good sir," I said, "you seem much stirred;
  The sacred compromises —"
"Now God confound the dastard word!
  My gall thereat arises:
Northward it hath this sense alone,
  That you, your conscience blinding,
Shall bow your fool's nose to the stone,
  When slavery feels like grinding.

"'T is shame to see such painted sticks
  In Vane's and Winthrop's places,
To see your spirit of Seventy-six
  Drag humbly in the traces,
With slavery's lash upon her back,
  And herds of office-holders
To shout applause, as, with a crack,
  It peels her patient shoulders.

"*We* forefathers to such a rout! —
  No, by my faith in God's word!"
Half rose the ghost, and half drew out
  The ghost of his old broadsword,
Then thrust it slowly back again,
  And said, with reverent gesture,
"No, Freedom, no! blood should not stain
  The hem of thy white vesture.

"I feel the soul in me draw near
  The mount of prophesying;
In this bleak wilderness I hear
  A John the Baptist crying;
Far in the east I see upleap
  The streaks of first forewarning,
And they who sowed the light shall reap
  The golden sheaves of morning.

"Child of our travail and our woe,
  Light in our day of sorrow,
Through my rapt spirit I foreknow
  The glory of thy morrow;
I hear great steps, that through the shade
  Draw nigher still and nigher,
And voices call like that which bade
  The prophet come up higher."

I looked, no form mine eyes could find,
  I heard the red cock crowing,
And through my window-chinks the wind
  A dismal tune was blowing ;
Thought I, My neighbor Buckingham
  Hath somewhat in him gritty,
Some Pilgrim-stuff that hates all sham,
  And he will print my ditty.

THE COURTIN'.

GOD makes sech nights, all white an still
  Fur 'z you can look or listen,
Moonshine an' snow on field an' hill,
  All silence an' all glisten.

Zekle crep' up quite unbeknown
  An' peeked in thru' the winder,
An' there sot Huldy all alone,
  'ith no one nigh to hender.

A fireplace filled the room's one side
  With half a cord o' wood in —

There warn't no stoves (tell comfort died)
 To bake ye to a puddin'.

The wa'nut logs shot sparkles out
 Towards the pootiest, bless her,
An' leetle flames danced all about
 The chiny on the dresser.

Agin the chimbley crook-necks hung,
 An' in amongst 'em rusted
The ole queen's-arm thet gran'ther Young
 Fetched back from Concord busted.

The very room, coz she was in,
 Seemed warm from floor to ceilin',
An' she looked full ez rosy agin
 Ez the apples she was peelin'.

'T was kin' o' kingdom-come to look
 On sech a blessed cretur,
A dogrose blushin' to a brook
 Ain't modester nor sweeter.

He was six foot o' man, A 1,
 Clear grit an' human natur';

None could n't quicker pitch a ton
  Nor dror a furrer straighter.

He 'd sparked it with full twenty gals,
  Hed squired 'em, danced 'em, druv 'em,
Fust this one, an' then thet, by spells —
  All is, he could n't love 'em.

But long o' her his veins 'ould run
  All crinkly like curled maple,
The side she breshed felt full o' sun
  Ez a south slope in Ap'il.

She thought no v'ice hed sech a swing
  Ez hisn in the choir;
My! when he made Ole Hunderd ring,
  She *knowed* the Lord was nigher.

An' she 'd blush scarlet, right in prayer,
  When her new meetin'-bunnet
Felt somehow thru' its crown a pair
  O' blue eyes sot upon it.

Thet night, I tell ye, she looked *some!*
  She seemed to 've gut a new soul,

For she felt sartin-sure he 'd come,
  Down to her very shoe-sole.

She heered a foot, an' knowed it tu,
  A-raspin' on the scraper, —
All ways to once her feelins flew
  Like sparks in burnt-up paper.

He kin' o' l'itered on the mat,
  Some doubtfle o' the sekle,
His heart kep' goin' pity-pat,
  But hern went pity Zekle.

An' yit she gin her cheer a jerk
  Ez though she wished him furder,
An' on her apples kep' to work,
  Parin' away like murder.

"You want to see my Pa, I s'pose?"
  "Wal . . . no . . . I come dasignin'" —
"To see my Ma? She 's sprinklin' clo'es
  Agin to-morrer's i'nin'."

To say why gals acts so or so,
  Or don't, 'ould be presumin';

Mebby to mean *yes* an' say *no*
  Comes nateral to women.

He stood a spell on one foot fust,
  Then stood a spell on t' other,
An' on which one he felt the wust
  He could n't ha' told ye nuther.

Says he, "I 'd better call agin";
  Says she, "Think likely, Mister":
Thet last word pricked him like a pin,
  An'... Wal, he up an' kist her.

When Ma bimeby upon 'em slips,
  Huldy sot pale ez ashes,
All kin' o' smily roun' the lips
  An' teary roun' the lashes.

For she was jes' the quiet kind
  Whose naturs never vary,
Like streams that keep a summer mind
  Snowhid in Jenooary.

The blood clost roun' her heart felt glued
  Too tight for all expressin',

"He stood a spell on one foot first,
Then stood a spell on t' other."

Tell mother see how metters stood,
  An' gin 'em both her blessin'.

Then her red come back like the tide
  Down to the Bay o' Fundy,
An' all I know is they was cried
  In meetin' come nex' Sunday.

WHAT MR. ROBINSON THINKS.

UVENER B. is a sensible man ;
  He stays to his home an' looks arter his folks ;
He draws his furrer ez straight ez he can,
  An' into nobody's tater-patch pokes ;
    But John P.
    Robinson he
  Sez he wunt vote fer Guvener B.

My ! aint it terrible ? Wut shall we du ?
  We can't never choose him o' course, — thet 's flat ;
Guess we shall hev to come round, (don't you ?)
  An' go in fer thunder an' guns, an' all that ;

Fer John P.
Robinson he
Sez he wunt vote fer Guvener B.

Gineral C. is a dreffle smart man :
He 's ben on all sides thet give places or pelf ;
But consistency still wuz a part of his plan, —
He 's ben true to *one* party, — an' thet is himself ; —
So John P.
Robinson he
Sez he shall vote fer Gineral C.

Gineral C. he goes in fer the war ;
He don't vally principle more 'n an old cud ;
Wut did God make us raytional creeturs fer,
But glory an' gunpowder, plunder an' blood ?
So John P.
Robinson he
Sez he shall vote fer Gineral C.

We were gittin' on nicely up here to our village,
With good old idees o' wut 's right an' wut aint,

We kind o' thought Christ went agin war an' pillage,
An' thet eppyletts worn't the best mark of a saint;
But John P.
Robinson he
Sez this kind o' thing 's an exploded idee.

The side of our country must ollers be took,
An' Presidunt Polk, you know, *he* is our country.
An' the angel thet writes all our sins in a book
Puts the *debit* to him, an' to us the *per contry;*
An' John P.
Robinson he
Sez this is his view o' the thing to a T.

Parson Wilbur he calls all these argimunts lies;
Sez they 're nothin' on airth but jest *fee, faw, fum:*
An' thet all this big talk of our destinies
Is half on it ign'ance, an' t' other half rum;
But John P.
Robinson he

Sez it aint no sech thing ; an', of course,
so must we.

Parson Wilbur sez *he* never heerd in his life
Thet th' Apostles rigged out in their swaller-tail coats,
An' marched round in front of a drum an' a fife,
To git some on 'em office, an' some on 'em votes ;
But John P.
Robinson he
Sez they did n't know everythin' down in Judee.

Wal, it 's a marcy we 've gut folks to tell us
The rights an' the wrongs o' these matters, I vow, —
God sends country lawyers, an' other wise fellers,
To start the world's team wen it gits in a slough ;
Fer John P.
Robinson he
Sez the world 'll go right, ef he hollers out Gee !

MR. HOSEA BIGLOW
TO THE EDITOR OF THE ATLANTIC MONTHLY.

EAR SIR, — Your letter come to han'
Requestin' me to please be funny ;
But I ain't made upon a plan
Thet knows wut 's comin', gall or honey :
Ther' 's times the world doos look so queer,
Odd fancies come afore I call 'em ;
An' then agin, for half a year,
No preacher 'thout a call 's more solemn.

You 're 'n want o' sunthin' light an' cute,
Rattlin' an' shrewd an' kin' o' jingleish,
An' wish, pervidin' it 'ould suit,
I 'd take an' citify my English.
I *ken* write long-tailed, ef I please, —
But when I 'm jokin', no, I thankee ;
Then, 'fore I know it, my idees
Run helter-skelter into Yankee.

Sence I begun to scribble rhyme,
I tell ye wut, I hain't ben foolin' ;
The parson's books, life, death, an' time
Hev took some trouble with my schoolin' ;

Nor th' airth don't git put out with me,
  Thet love her 'z though she wuz a woman ;
Why, th' ain't a bird upon the tree
  But half forgives my bein' human.

An' yit I love th' unhighschooled way
  Ol' farmers hed when I wuz younger ;
Their talk wuz meatier, an' 'ould stay,
  While book-froth seems to whet your hunger ;
For puttin' in a downright lick
  'twixt Humbug's eyes, ther' 's few can metch it,
An' then it helves my thoughts ez slick
  Ez stret-grained hickory doos a hetchet.

But when I can't, I can't, thet 's all,
  For Natur' won't put up with gullin' ;
Idees you hev to shove an' haul
  Like a druv pig ain't wuth a mullein :
Live thoughts ain't sent for ; thru all rifts
  O' sense they pour an' resh ye onwards,
Like rivers when south-lyin' drifts
  Feel thet th' old airth 's a-wheelin' sunwards.

Time wuz, the rhymes come crowdin' thick
  Ez office-seekers arter 'lection,
An' into ary place 'ould stick
  Without no bother nor objection ;
But sence the war my thoughts hang back
  Ez though I wanted to enlist 'em,
An' subs'tutes, — *they* don't never lack,
  But then they'll slope afore you've mist 'em.

Nothin' don't seem like wut it wuz ;
  I can't see wut there is to hender,
An' yit my brains jes' go buzz, buzz,
  Like bumblebees agin a winder ;
'Fore these times come, in all airth's row,
  Ther' wuz one quiet place, my head in,
Where I could hide an' think, — but now
  It's all one teeter, hopin', dreadin'.

Where's Peace ? I start, some clear-blown night,
  When gaunt stone walls grow numb an' number,
An', creakin' 'cross the snow-crus' white,
  Walk the col' starlight into summer ;

Up grows the moon, an' swell by swell
  Thru the pale pasturs silvers dimmer
Than the last smile thet strives to tell
  O' love gone heavenward in its shimmer.

I hev ben gladder o' sech things
  Than cocks o' spring or bees o' clover,
They filled my heart with livin' springs,
  But now they seem to freeze 'em over ;
Sights innercent ez babes on knee,
  Peaceful ez eyes o' pastur'd cattle,
Jes' coz they be so, seem to me
  To rile me more with thoughts o' battle.

In-doors an' out by spells I try ;
  Ma'am Natur' keeps her spin-wheel goin'.
But leaves my natur' stiff and dry
  Ez fiel's o' clover arter mowin' ;
An' her jes' keepin' on the same,
  Calmer 'n a clock, an' never carin',
An' findin' nary thing to blame,
  Is wus than ef she took to swearin'.

Snow-flakes come whisperin' on the pane
  The charm makes blazin' logs so pleasant,

But I can't hark to wut they 're say'n',
With Grant or Sherman ollers present ;
The chimbleys shudder in the gale,
Thet lulls, then suddin takes to flappin'
Like a shot hawk, but all 's ez stale
To me ez so much sperit-rappin'.

Under the yaller-pines I house,
When sunshine makes 'em all sweet-scented,
An' hear among their furry boughs
The baskin' west-wind purr contented,
While 'way o'erhead, ez sweet an' low
Ez distant bells thet ring for meetin',
The wedged wil' geese their bugles blow,
Further an' further South retreatin'.

Or up the slippery knob I strain
An' see a hundred hills like islan's
Lift their blue woods in broken chain
Out o' the sea o' snowy silence ;
The farm-smokes, sweetes' sight on airth,
Slow thru the winter air a-shrinkin'
Seem kin' o' sad, an' roun' the hearth
Of empty places set me thinkin'.

Beaver roars hoarse with meltin' snows,
  An' rattles di'mon's from his granite ;
Time wuz, he snatched away my prose,
  An' into psalms or satires ran it ;
But he, nor all the rest thet once
  Started my blood to country-dances,
Can't set me goin' more 'n a dunce
  Thet hain't no use for dreams an' fancies.

Rat-tat-tat-tattle thru the street
  I hear the drummers makin' riot,
An' I set thinkin' o' the feet
  Thet follered once an' now are quiet, —
White feet ez snowdrops innercent,
  Thet never knowed the paths o' Satan,
Whose comin' step ther' 's ears thet won't,
  No, not lifelong, leave off awaitin'.

Why, hain't I held 'em on my knee ?
  Did n't I love to see 'em growin',
Three likely lads ez wal could be,
  Hahnsome an' brave an' not tu knowin' ?
I set an' look into the blaze
  Whose natur', jes' like theirn, keeps climb-
    in',

Ez long 'z it lives, in shinin' ways,
  An' half despise myself for rhymin'.

Wut 's words to them whose faith an' truth
  On War's red techstone rang true metal,
Who ventered life an' love an' youth
  For the gret prize o' death in battle?
To him who, deadly hurt, agen
  Flashed on afore the charge's thunder,
Tippin' with fire the bolt of men
  Thet rived the Rebel line asunder?

'T ain't right to hev the young go fust,
  All throbbin' full o' gifts an' graces,
Leavin' life's paupers dry ez dust
  To try an' make b'lieve fill their places:
Nothin' but tells us wut we miss,
  Ther' 's gaps our lives can't never fay in,
An' *thet* world seems so fur from this
  Lef' for us loafers to grow gray in!

My eyes cloud up for rain; my mouth
  Will take to twitchin' roun' the corners;
I pity mothers, tu, down South,
  For all they sot among the scorners:

I 'd sooner take my chance to stan'
  At Jedgment where your meanest slave is,
Than at God's bar hol' up a han'
  Ez drippin' red ez yourn, Jeff Davis!

Come, Peace! not like a mourner bowed
  For honor lost an' dear ones wasted,
But proud, to meet a people proud,
  With eyes thet tell o' triumph tasted!
Come, with han' grippin' on the hilt,
  An' step thet proves ye Victory's daughter!
Longin' for you, our sperits wilt
  Like shipwrecked men's on raf's for water.

Come, while our country feels the lift
  Of a gret instinct shoutin' forwards,
An' knows thet freedom ain't a gift
  Thet tarries long in han's o' cowards!
Come, sech ez mothers prayed for, when
  They kissed their cross with lips thet quiv-
    ered,
An' bring fair wages for brave men,
  A nation saved, a race delivered!

TO CHARLES ELIOT NORTON.

AGRO DOLCE.

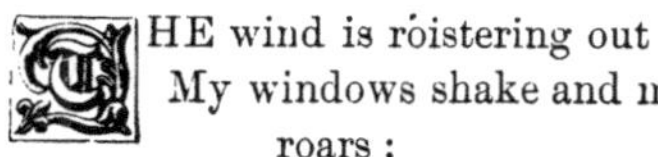
HE wind is roistering out of doors,
  My windows shake and my chimney
      roars;
My Elmwood chimneys seem crooning to me,
As of old, in their moody, minor key,
And out of the past the hoarse wind blows,
As I sit in my arm-chair, and toast my toes.

"Ho! ho! nine-and-forty," they seem to sing,
"We saw you a little toddling thing.
We knew you child and youth and man,
A wonderful fellow to dream and plan,
With a great thing always to come, — who
    knows?
Well, well! 't is some comfort to toast one's
    toes.

"How many times have you sat at gaze
Till the mouldering fire forgot to blaze,
Shaping among the whimsical coals

Fancies and figures and shining goals !
What matters the ashes that cover those ?
While hickory lasts you can toast your toes.

" O dream-ship-builder ! where are they all,
Your grand three-deckers, deep-chested and
tall,
That should crush the waves under canvas
piles,
And anchor at last by the Fortunate Isles ?
There 's gray in your beard, the years turn
foes,
While you muse in your arm-chair, and toast
your toes."

I sit and dream that I hear, as of yore,
My Elmwood chimneys' deep-throated roar;
If much be gone, there is much remains ;
By the embers of loss I count my gains,
You and yours with the best, till the old
hope glows
In the fanciful flame, as I toast my toes.

Instead of a fleet of broad-browed ships,
To send a child's armada of chips !

Instead of the great guns, tier on tier,
A freight of pebbles and grass-blades sere!
"Well, maybe more love with the less gift goes,"
I growl, as, half moody, I toast my toes.

THE FIRST SNOW-FALL.

THE snow had begun in the gloaming,
And busily all the night
Had been heaping field and highway
With a silence deep and white.

Every pine and fir and hemlock
Wore ermine too dear for an earl,
And the poorest twig on the elm-tree
Was ridged inch deep with pearl.

From sheds new-roofed with Carrara
Came Chanticleer's muffled crow,
The stiff rails were softened to swan's-down,
And still fluttered down the snow.

I stood and watched by the window
The noiseless work of the sky,

And the sudden flurries of snow-birds,
  Like brown leaves whirling by.

I thought of a mound in sweet Auburn
  Where a little headstone stood;
How the flakes were folding it gently,
  As did robins the babes in the wood.

Up spoke our own little Mabel,
  Saying, "Father, who makes it snow?"
And I told of the good All-father
  Who cares for us here below.

Again I looked at the snow-fall,
  And thought of the leaden sky
That arched o'er our first great sorrow,
  When that mound was heaped so high.

I remembered the gradual patience
  That fell from that cloud like snow,
Flake by flake, healing and hiding
  The scar of our deep-plunged woe.

And again to the child I whispered,
  "The snow that husheth all,

"With eyes that saw not I kissed her."

Darling, the merciful Father
  Alone can make it fall!"

Then, with eyes that saw not, I kissed her;
  And she, kissing back, could not know
That *my* kiss was given to her sister,
  Folded close under deepening snow.

WITHOUT AND WITHIN.

Y coachman, in the moonlight there,
  Looks through the side-light of the door;
I hear him with his brethren swear,
  As I could do, — but only more.

Flattening his nose against the pane,
  He envies me my brilliant lot,
Breathes on his aching fists in vain,
  And dooms me to a place more hot.

He sees me in to supper go,
  A silken wonder by my side,
Bare arms, bare shoulders, and a row
  Of flounces, for the door too wide.

He thinks how happy is my arm
  'Neath its white-gloved and jewelled load;
And wishes me some dreadful harm,
  Hearing the merry corks explode.

Meanwhile I inly curse the bore
  Of hunting still the same old coon,
And envy him, outside the door,
  In golden quiets of the moon.

The winter wind is not so cold
  As the bright smile he sees me win,
Nor the host's oldest wine so old
  As our poor gabble sour and thin.

I envy him the ungyved prance
  By which his freezing feet he warms,
And drag my lady's-chains and dance
  The galley-slave of dreary forms.

O, could he have my share of din,
  And I his quiet! — past a doubt
'T would still be one man bored within,
  And just another bored without.

GODMINSTER CHIMES.

WRITTEN IN AID OF A CHIME OF BELLS FOR CHRIST CHURCH, CAMBRIDGE.

GODMINSTER? Is it Fancy's play?
I know not, but the word
Sings in my heart, nor can I say
Whether 't was dreamed or heard;
Yet fragrant in my mind it clings
As blossoms after rain,
And builds of half-remembered things
This vision in my brain.

Through aisles of long-drawn centuries
My spirit walks in thought,
And to that symbol lifts its eyes
Which God's own pity wrought;
From Calvary shines the altar's gleam,
The Church's East is there,
The Ages one great minster seem,
That throbs with praise and prayer.

And all the way from Calvary down
The carven pavement shows

Their graves who won the martyr's crown
  And safe in God repose ;
The saints of many a warring creed
  Who now in heaven have learned
That all paths to the Father lead
  Where Self the feet have spurned.

And, as the mystic aisles I pace,
  By aureoled workmen built,
Lives ending at the Cross I trace
  Alike through grace and guilt ;
One Mary bathes the blessed feet
  With ointment from her eyes,
With spikenard one, and both are sweet,
  For both are sacrifice.

Moravian hymn and Roman chant
  In one devotion blend,
To speak the soul's eternal want
  Of Him, the inmost friend ;
One prayer soars cleansed with martyr fire,
  One choked with sinner's tears,
In heaven both meet in one desire,
  And God one music hears.

Whilst thus I dream, the bells clash out
  Upon the Sabbath air,
Each seems a hostile faith to shout,
  A selfish form of prayer ;
My dream is shattered, yet who knows
  But in that heaven so near
These discords find harmonious close
  In God's atoning ear ?

O chime of sweet Saint Charity,
  Peal soon that Easter morn
When Christ for all shall risen be,
  And in all hearts new-born !
That Pentecost when utterance clear
  To all men shall be given,
When all shall say *My Brother* here,
  And hear *My Son* in heaven !

AUF WIEDERSEHEN!

SUMMER.

THE little gate was reached at last,
  Half hid in lilacs down the lane ;
  She pushed it wide, and, as she past,
A wistful look she backward cast,
  And said, — "*Auf Wiedersehen!*"

With hand on latch, a vision white
  Lingered reluctant, and again
Half doubting if she did aright,
Soft as the dews that fell that night,
  She said, — "*Auf Wiedersehen!*"

The lamp's clear gleam flits up the stair;
  I linger in delicious pain;
Ah, in that chamber, whose rich air
To breathe in thought I scarcely dare,
  Thinks she, — "*Auf Wiedersehen!*"

'T is thirteen years; once more I press
  The turf that silences the lane;
I hear the rustle of her dress,
I smell the lilacs, and — ah, yes,
  I hear "*Auf Wiedersehen!*"

Sweet piece of bashful maiden art!
  The English words had seemed too fain,
But these — they drew us heart to heart,
Yet held us tenderly apart;
  She said, "*Auf Wiedersehen!*"

PALINODE.

WINTER.

STILL thirteen years: 't is autumn now
  On field and hill, in heart and brain;
The naked trees at evening sough;
The leaf to the forsaken bough
  Sighs not, — "We meet again!"

Two watched yon oriole's pendent dome,
  That now is void, and dank with rain,
And one, — O, hope more frail than foam!
The bird to his deserted home
  Sings not, — "We meet again!"

The loath gate swings with rusty creak;
  Once, parting there, we played at pain;
There came a parting, when the weak
And fading lips essayed to speak
  Vainly, — "We meet again!"

Somewhere is comfort, somewhere faith,
  Though thou in outer dark remain;

One sweet sad voice ennobles death,
And still, for eighteen centuries saith
Softly, — "Ye meet again!"

If earth another grave must bear,
Yet heaven hath won a sweeter strain,
And something whispers my despair,
That, from an orient chamber there,
Floats down, "We meet again!"

AFTER THE BURIAL.

YES, faith is a goodly anchor;
When skies are sweet as a psalm,
At the bows it lolls so stalwart,
In bluff, broad-shouldered calm.

And when over breakers to leeward
The tattered surges are hurled,
It may keep our head to the tempest,
With its grip on the base of the world.

But, after the shipwreck, tell me
What help in its iron thews,

Still true to the broken hawser,
Deep down among sea-weed and ooze ?

In the breaking gulfs of sorrow,
When the helpless feet stretch out
And find in the deeps of darkness
No footing so solid as doubt,

Then better one spar of Memory,
One broken plank of the Past,
That our human heart may cling to,
Though hopeless of shore at last !

To the spirit its splendid conjectures,
To the flesh its sweet despair,
Its tears o'er the thin-worn locket
With its anguish of deathless hair !

Immortal ? I feel it and know it,
Who doubts it of such as she ?
But that is the pang's very secret, —
Immortal away from me.

There 's a narrow ridge in the graveyard
Would scarce stay a child in his race,

But to me and my thought it is wider
Than the star-sown vague of Space.

Your logic, my friend, is perfect,
Your morals most drearily true ;
But, since the earth clashed on *her* coffin,
I keep hearing that, and not you.

Console if you will, I can bear it ;
'T is a well-meant alms of breath ;
But not all the preaching since Adam
Has made Death other than Death.

It is pagan ; but wait till you feel it, —
That jar of our earth, that dull shock
When the ploughshare of deeper passion
Tears down to our primitive rock.

Communion in spirit! Forgive me,
But I, who am earthy and weak,
Would give all my incomes from dreamland
For a touch of her hand on my cheek.

That little shoe in the corner,
So worn and wrinkled and brown,
With its emptiness confutes you,
And argues your wisdom down.

THE DEAD HOUSE.

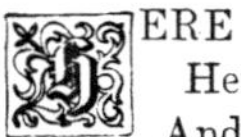ERE once my step was quickened,
Here beckoned the opening door,
And welcome thrilled from the threshold
To the foot it had known before.

A glow came forth to meet me
From the flame that laughed in the grate,
And shadows adance on the ceiling,
Danced blither with mine for a mate.

"I claim you, old friend," yawned the arm-chair,
"This corner, you know, is your seat";
"Rest your slippers on me," beamed the fender,
"I brighten at touch of your feet."

"We know the practised finger,"
Said the books, "that seems like brain";
And the shy page rustled the secret
It had kept till I came again.

Sang the pillow, " My down once quivered
  On nightingale's throats that flew
Through moonlit gardens of Hafiz
  To gather quaint dreams for you."

Ah me, where the Past sowed heart's-ease,
  The Present plucks rue for us men!
I come back: that scar unhealing
  Was not in the churchyard then.

But, I think, the house is unaltered,
  I will go and beg to look
At the rooms that were once familiar
  To my life as its bed to a brook.

Unaltered! Alas for the sameness
  That makes the change but more!
'T is a dead man I see in the mirrors,
  'T is his tread that chills the floor!

To learn such a simple lesson,
  Need I go to Paris and Rome,
That the many make the household,
  But only one the home?

'T was just a womanly presence,
  An influence unexprest,

But a rose she had worn, on my grave-sod
Were more than long life with the rest!

'T was a smile, 't was a garment's rustle,
'T was nothing that I can phrase,
But the whole dumb dwelling grew conscious,
And put on her looks and ways.

Were it mine I would close the shutters,
Like lids when the life is fled,
And the funeral fire should wind it,
This corpse of a home that is dead.

For it died that autumn morning
When she, its soul, was borne
To lie all dark on the hillside
That looks over woodland and corn.

YUSSOUF.

STRANGER came one night to Yussouf's tent,
Saying, "Behold one outcast and in dread,

Against whose life the bow of power is bent,
Who flies, and hath not where to lay his
head;
I come to thee for shelter and for food,
To Yussouf, called through all our tribes
'The Good.'"

"This tent is mine," said Yussouf, "but no
more
Than it is God's; come in, and be at peace;
Freely shalt thou partake of all my store
As I of His who buildeth over these
Our tents his glorious roof of night and day,
And at whose door none ever yet heard Nay."

So Yussouf entertained his guest that night,
And, waking him ere day, said: "Here is
gold;
My swiftest horse is saddled for thy flight;
Depart before the prying day grow bold."
As one lamp lights another, nor grows less,
So nobleness enkindleth nobleness.

That inward light the stranger's face made
grand,

Which shines from all self-cónquest; kneel-
ing low,
He bowed his forehead upon Yussouf's hand,
Sobbing: "O Sheik, I cannot leave thee so;
I will repay thee; all this thou hast done
Unto that Ibrahim who slew thy son!"

"Take thrice the gold," said Yussouf, "for
with thee
Into the desert, never to return,
My one black thought shall ride away from
me;
First-born, for whom by day and night I
yearn,
Balanced and just are all of God's decrees;
Thou art avenged, my first-born, sleep in
peace!"

WHAT RABBI JEHOSHA SAID.

ABBI JEHOSHA used to say
That God made angels every day,
Perfect as Michael and the rest
First brooded in creation's nest,

Whose only office was to cry
Hosanna! once, and then to die;
Or rather, with Life's essence blent,
To be led home from banishment.

Rabbi Jehosha had the skill
To know that Heaven is in God's will;
And doing that, though for a space
One heart-beat long, may win a grace
As full of grandeur and of glow
As Princes of the Chariot know.

'T were glorious, no doubt, to be
One of the strong-winged Hierarchy,
To burn with Seraphs, or to shine
With Cherubs, deathlessly divine;
Yet I, perhaps, poor earthly clod,
Could I forget myself in God,
Could I but find my nature's clew
Simply as birds and blossoms do,
And but for one rapt moment know
'T is Heaven must come, not we must go,
Should win my place as near the throne
As the pearl-angel of its zone,
And God would listen mid the throng

For my one breath of perfect song,
That, in its simple human way,
Said all the Host of Heaven could say.

ALL-SAINTS.

NE feast, of holy days the crest,
I, though no Churchman, love to keep,
All-Saints, — the unknown good that rest
In God's still memory folded deep;
The bravely dumb that did their deed,
And scorned to blot it with a name,
Men of the plain heroic breed,
That loved Heaven's silence more than fame.

Such lived not in the past alone,
But thread to-day the unheeding street,
And stairs to Sin and Famine known
Sing with the welcome of their feet;
The den they enter grows a shrine,
The grimy sash an oriel burns,
Their cup of water warms like wine,
Their speech is filled from heavenly urns.

About their brows to me appears
An aureole traced in tenderest light,
The rainbow-gleam of smiles through tears
In dying eyes, by them made bright,
Of souls that shivered on the edge
Of that chill ford repassed no more,
And in their mercy felt the pledge
And sweetness of the farther shore.

THE DARKENED MIND.

HE fire is burning clear and blithely,
Pleasantly whistles the winter wind ;
We are about thee, thy friends and kindred,
On us all flickers the firelight kind ;
There thou sitt'st in thy wonted corner
Lone and awful in thy darkened mind.

There thou sitt'st ; now and then thou moanest ;
Thou dost talk with what we cannot see,
Lookest at us with an eye so doubtful,
It doth put us very far from thee ;

There thou sittest ; we would fain be nigh
thee,
But we know that it can never be.

We can touch thee, still we are no nearer ;
Gather round thee, still thou art alone ;
The wide chasm of reason is between us ;
Thou confutest kindness with a moan ;
We can speak to thee, and thou canst answer,
Like two prisoners through a wall of stone.

Hardest heart would call it very awful
When thou look'st at us and seest — O,
what ?
If we move away, thou sittest gazing
With those vague eyes at the selfsame spot,
And thou mutterest, thy hands thou wringest
Seeing something, — us thou seëst not.

Strange it is that, in this open brightness,
Thou shouldst sit in such a narrow cell ;
Strange it is that thou shouldst be so lone-
some
Where those are who love thee all so well ;
Not so much of thee is left among us
As the hum outliving the hushed bell.

AN EMBER PICTURE.

HOW strange are the freaks of memory !
The lessons of life we forget,
While a trifle, a trick of color,
In the wonderful web is set, —

Set by some mordant of fancy,
And, spite of the wear and tear
Of time or distance or trouble,
Insists on its right to be there.

A chance had brought us together ;
Our talk was of matters-of-course ;
We were nothing, one to the other,
But a short half-hour's resource.

We spoke of French acting and actors,
And their easy, natural way :
Of the weather, for it was raining
As we drove home from the play.

We debated the social nothings
We bore ourselves so to discuss ;

The thunderous rumors of battle
  Were silent the while for us.

Arrived at her door, we left her
  With a drippingly hurried adieu,
And our wheels went crunching the gravel
  Of the oak-darkened avenue.

As we drove away through the shadow,
  The candle she held in the door
From rain-varnished tree-trunk to tree-trunk
  Flashed fainter, and flashed no more ; —

Flashed fainter, then wholly faded
  Before we had passed the wood ;
But the light of the face behind it
  Went with me and stayed for good.

The vision of scarce a moment,
  And hardly marked at the time,
It comes unbidden to haunt me,
  Like a scrap of ballad-rhyme.

Had she beauty ? Well, not what they call so ;
  You may find a thousand as fair ;

And yet there 's her face in my memory
With no special claim to be there.

As I sit sometimes in the twilight,
And call back to life in the coals
Old faces and hopes and fancies
Long buried, (good rest to their souls!)

Her face shines out in the embers;
I see her holding the light,
And hear the crunch of the gravel
And the sweep of the rain that night.

'T is a face that can never grow older,
That never can part with its gleam,
'T is a gracious possession forever,
For is it not all a dream?

TO H. W. L.

ON HIS BIRTHDAY, 27TH FEBRUARY, 1867.

NEED not praise the sweetness of his song,
Where limpid verse to limpid verse succeeds

Smooth as our Charles, when, fearing lest he
wrong
The new moon's mirrored skiff, he slides along,
Full without noise, and whispers in his
reeds.

With loving breath of all the winds his name
Is blown about the world, but to his friends
A sweeter secret hides behind his fame,
And Love steals shyly through the loud
acclaim
To murmur a *God bless you!* and there ends.

As I muse backward up the checkered years
Wherein so much was given, so much was
lost,
Blessings in both kinds, such as cheapen
tears, —
But hush! this is not for profaner ears;
Let them drink molten pearls nor dream
the cost.

Some suck up poison from a sorrow's core,
As naught but nightshade grew upon earth's
ground;

Love turned all his to heart's-ease, and the
more
Fate tried his bastions, she but forced a door
Leading to sweeter manhood and more
sound.

Even as a wind-wáved fountain's swaying
shade
Seems of mixed race, a gray wraith shot
with sun,
So through his trial faith translucent rayed
Till darkness, half disnatured so, betrayed
A heart of sunshine that would fain o'errun.

Surely if skill in song the shears may stay
And of its purpose cheat the charmed abyss,
If our poor life be lengthened by a lay,
He shall not go, although his presence may,
And the next age in praise shall double this.

Long days be his, and each as lusty-sweet
As gracious natures find his song to be;
May Age steal on with softly-cadenced feet
Falling in music, as for him were meet
Whose choicest verse is harsher-toned than
he!

THE NIGHTINGALE IN THE STUDY.

OME forth!" my catbird calls to me,
"And hear me sing a cavatina
That, in this old familiar tree,
Shall hang a garden of Alcina.

"These buttercups shall brim with wine
Beyond all Lesbian juice or Massic;
May not New England be divine?
My ode to ripening summer classic?

"Or, if to me you will not hark,
By Beaver Brook a thrush is ringing
Till all the alder-coverts dark
Seem sunshine-dappled with his singing.

"Come out beneath the unmastered sky,
With its emancipating spaces,
And learn to sing as well as I,
Without premeditated graces.

"What boot your many-volumed gains,
Those withered leaves forever turning,

To win, at best, for all your pains,
  A nature mummy-wrapt in learning?

"The leaves wherein true wisdom lies
  On living trees the sun are drinking;
Those white clouds, drowsing through the skies,
  Grew not so beautiful by thinking.

"Come out! with me the oriole cries,
  Escape the demon that pursues you!
And, hark, the cuckoo weatherwise,
  Still hiding, farther onward wooes you."

"Alas, dear friend, that, all my days,
  Has poured from that syringa thicket
The quaintly discontinuous lays
  To which I hold a season-ticket,

"A season-ticket cheaply bought
  With a dessert of pilfered berries,
And who so oft my soul hast caught
  With morn and evening voluntaries,

"Deem me not faithless, if all day
  Among my dusty books I linger,

No pipe, like thee, for June to play
  With fancy-led, half-conscious finger.

"A bird is singing in my brain
  And bubbling o'er with mingled fancies,
Gay, tragic, rapt, right heart of Spain
  Fed with the sap of old romances.

"I ask no ampler skies than those
  His magic music rears above me,
No falser friends, no truer foes, —
  And does not Doña Clara love me?

"Cloaked shapes, a twanging of guitars,
  A rush of feet, and rapiers clashing,
Then silence deep with breathless stars,
  And overhead a white hand flashing.

"O music of all moods and climes,
  Vengeful, forgiving, sensuous, saintly,
Where still, between the Christian chimes,
  The Moorish cymbal tinkles faintly!

"O life borne lightly in the hand,
  For friend or foe with grace Castilian!
O valley safe in Fancy's land,
  Not tramped to mud yet by the million!

"Bird of to-day, thy songs are stale
  To his, my singer of all weathers,
My Calderon, my nightingale,
  My Arab soul in Spanish feathers.

"Ah, friend, these singers dead so long,
  And still, God knows, in purgatory,
Give its best sweetness to all song,
  To Nature's self her better glory."

IN THE TWILIGHT.

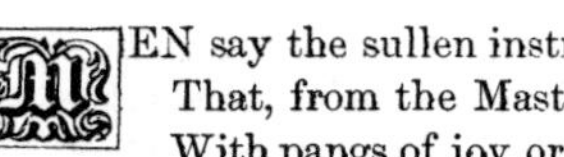
EN say the sullen instrument,
    That, from the Master's bow,
    With pangs of joy or woe,
Feels music's soul through every fibre sent,
  Whispers the ravished strings
More than he knew or meant;
  Old summers in its memory glow;
  The secrets of the wind it sings;
  It hears the April-loosened springs;
  And mixes with its mood
  All it dreamed when it stood
  In the murmurous pine-wood
        Long ago!

The magical moonlight then
  Steeped every bough and cone ;
The roar of the brook in the glen
  Came dim from the distance blown ;
The wind through its glooms sang low,
  And it swayed to and fro
    With delight as it stood,
    In the wonderful wood,
        Long ago !

O my life, have we not had seasons
  That only said, Live and rejoice ?
That asked not for causes and reasons,
  But made us all feeling and voice ?
When we went with the winds in their blowing,
  When Nature and we were peers,
And we seemed to share in the flowing
  Of the inexhaustible years ?
  Have we not from the earth drawn juices
  Too fine for earth's sordid uses ?
    Have I heard, have I seen
      All I feel and I know ?
    Doth my heart overween ?
    Or could it have been
        Long ago ?

Sometimes a breath floats by me,
  An odor from Dreamland sent,
That makes the ghost seem nigh me
  Of a splendor that came and went,
Of a life lived somewhere, I know not
  In what diviner sphere,
Of memories that stay not and go not,
  Like music heard once by an ear
    That cannot forget or reclaim it,
    A something so shy, it would shame it
      To make it a show,
    A something too vague, could I name it,
      For others to know,
    As if I had lived it or dreamed it,
    As if I had acted or schemed it,
            Long ago!

And yet, could I live it over,
  This life that stirs in my brain,
  Could I be both maiden and lover,
  Moon and tide, bee and clover,
    As I seem to have been, once again,
  Could I but speak and show it,
    This pleasure more sharp than pain,
      That baffles and lures me so,

The world should not lack a poet,
Such as it had
In the ages glad,
Long ago!

THE FOOT-PATH.

T mounts athwart the windy hill
Through sallow slopes of upland bare,
And Fancy climbs with foot-fall still
Its narrowing curves that end in air.

By day, a warmer-hearted blue
Stoops softly to that topmost swell;
Its thread-like windings seem a clew
To gracious climes where all is well.

By night, far yonder, I surmise
An ampler world than clips my ken,
Where the great stars of happier skies
Commingle nobler fates of men.

I look and long, then haste me home,
Still master of my secret rare;
Once tried, the path would end in Rome,
But now it leads me everywhere.

Forever to the new it guides,
  From former good, old overmuch;
What Nature for her poets hides,
  'T is wiser to divine than clutch.

The bird I list hath never come
  Within the scope of mortal ear;
My prying step would make him dumb,
  And the fair tree, his shelter, sear.

Behind the hill, behind the sky,
  Behind my inmost thought, he sings;
No feet avail; to hear it nigh,
  The song itself must lend the wings.

Sing on, sweet bird close hid, and raise
  Those angel stairways in my brain,
That climb from these low-vaulted days
  To spacious sunshines far from pain.

Sing when thou wilt, enchantment fleet,
  I leave thy covert haunt untrod,
And envy Science not her feat
  To make a twice-told tale of God.

They said the fairies tript no more,
  And long ago that Pan was dead;

'T was but that fools preferred to bore
  Earth's rind inch-deep for truth instead.

Pan leaps and pipes all summer long,
  The fairies dance each full-mooned night,
Would we but doff our lenses strong,
  And trust our wiser eyes' delight.

City of Elf-land, just without
  Our seeing, marvel ever new,
Glimpsed in fair weather, a sweet doubt
  Sketched-in, mirage-like, on the blue.

I build thee in yon sunset cloud,
  Whose edge allures to climb the height;
I hear thy drowned bells, inly-loud,
  From still pools dusk with dreams of night.

Thy gates are shut to hardiest will,
  Thy countersign of long-lost speech, —
Those fountained courts, those chambers still,
  Fronting Time's far East, who shall reach?

I know not, and will never pry,
  But trust our human heart for all;
Wonders that from the seeker fly
  Into an open sense may fall.

Hide in thine own soul, and surprise
The password of the unwary elves;
Seek it, thou canst not bribe their spies;
Unsought, they whisper it themselves.

THE WASHERS OF THE SHROUD.

OCTOBER, 1861.

LONG a river-side, I know not where,
I walked one night in mystery of dream;
A chill creeps curdling yet beneath my hair,
To think what chanced me by the pallid gleam
Of a moon-wraith that waned through haunted air.

Pale fireflies pulsed within the meadow-mist
Their halos, wavering thistledowns of light;
The loon, that seemed to mock some goblin tryst,
Laughed; and the echoes, huddling in affright,
Like Odin's hounds, fled baying down the night.

Then all was silent, till there smote my ear
A movement in the stream that checked my
breath :
Was it the slow plash of a wading deer?
But something said, " This water is of Death!
The Sisters wash a shroud, — ill thing to
hear! "

I, looking then, beheld the ancient Three
Known to the Greek's and to the North-
man's creed,
That sit in shadow of the mystic Tree,
Still crooning, as they weave their endless
brede,
One song : " Time was, Time is, and Time
shall be."

No wrinkled crones were they, as I had
deemed,
But fair as yesterday, to-day, to-morrow,
To mourner, lover, poet, ever seemed ;
Something too high for joy, too deep for
sorrow,
Thrilled in their tones, and from their faces
gleamed.

"Still men and nations reap as they have
strawn,"
So sang they, working at their task the while;
"The fatal raiment must be cleansed ere
dawn:
For Austria? Italy? the Sea-Queen's isle?
O'er what quenched grandeur must our
shroud be drawn?

"Or is it for a younger, fairer corse,
That gathered States like children round his
knees,
That tamed the wave to be his posting-horse,
Feller of forests, linker of the seas,
Bridge-builder, hammerer, youngest son of
Thor's?

"What make we, murmur'st thou? and what
are we?
When empires must be wound, we bring the
shroud,
The time-old web of the implacable Three:
Is it too coarse for him, the young and proud?
Earth's mightiest deigned to wear it, — why
not he?

"Is there no hope?" I moaned, "so strong, so
fair!
Our Fowler whose proud bird would brook
erewhile
No rival's swoop in all our western air!
Gather the ravens, then, in funeral file
For him, life's morn yet golden in his hair?

"Leave me not hopeless, ye unpitying dames!
I see, half seeing. Tell me, ye who scanned
The stars, Earth's elders, still must noblest
aims
Be traced upon oblivious ocean-sands?
Must Hesper join the wailing ghosts of
names?"

"When grass-blades stiffen with red battle-
dew,
Ye deem we choose the victor and the slain;
Say, choose we them that shall be leal and
true
To the heart's longing, the high faith of brain?
Yet there the victory lies, if ye but knew.

"Three roots bear up Dominion: Knowledge,
Will, —

These twain are strong, but stronger yet the
third, —
Obedience, — 'tis the great tap-root that
still,
Knit round the rock of Duty, is not stirred,
Though Heaven-loosed tempests spend their
utmost skill.

"Is the doom sealed for Hesper? 'T is not we
Denounce it, but the Law before all time:
The brave makes danger opportunity;
The waverer, paltering with the chance sub-
lime,
Dwarfs it to peril: which shall Hesper be?

"Hath he let vultures climb his eagle's seat
To make Jove's bolts purveyors of their maw?
Hath he the Many's plaudits found more sweet
Than Wisdom? held Opinion's wind for Law?
Then let him hearken for the doomster's feet!

"Rough are the steps, slow-hewn in flintiest
rock,
States climb to power by; slippery those with
gold

Down which they stumble to eternal mock :
No chafferer's hand shall long the sceptre hold,
Who, given a Fate to shape, would sell the
block.

"We sing old Sagas, songs of weal and woe,
Mystic because too cheaply understood ;
Dark sayings are not ours ; men hear and
know,
See Evil weak, see strength alone in Good,
Yet hope to stem God's fire with walls of tow.

"Time Was unlocks the riddle of Time Is,
That offers choice of glory or of gloom ;
The solver makes Time Shall Be surely his.
But hasten, Sisters ! for even now the tomb
Grates its slow hinge and calls from the abyss."

"But not for him," I cried, "not yet for him,
Whose large horizon, westering, star by star
Wins from the void to where on Ocean's rim
The sunset shuts the world with golden bar,
Not yet his thews shall fail, his eye grow dim !

"His shall be larger manhood, saved for those
That walk unblenching through the trial-fires ;
Not suffering, but faint heart, is worst of woes,

And he no base-born son of craven sires,
Whose eye need blench confronted with his
foes.

" Tears may be ours, but proud, for those who
win
Death's royal purple in the foeman's lines ;
Peace, too, brings tears ; and mid the battle-
din,
The wiser ear some text of God divines,
For the sheathed blade may rust with darker
sin.
" God, give us peace ! not such as lulls to sleep,
But sword on thigh, and brow with purpose
knit !
And let our Ship of State to harbor sweep,
Her ports all up, her battle-lanterns lit,
And her leashed thunders gathering for their
leap ! "

So cried I with clenched hands and passion-
ate pain,
Thinking of dear ones by Potomac's side ;
Again the loon laughed mocking, and again
The echoes bayed far down the night and died,
While waking I recalled my wandering brain.

www.ingramcontent.com/pod-product-compliance
Lightning Source LLC
LaVergne TN
LVHW010233110826
845151LV00004B/1280

* 9 7 8 1 4 2 5 5 2 4 7 4 6 *